Speaking Hope

Speaking Hope

The Body of Christ and Pastoral Counseling

Jack Holland

RESOURCE *Publications* • Eugene, Oregon

SPEAKING HOPE
The Body of Christ and Pastoral Counseling

Copyright © 2019 Jack Holland. All rights reserved. Except for brief quotations in critical publications or reviews, no part of this book may be reproduced in any manner without prior written permission from the publisher. Write: Permissions, Wipf and Stock Publishers, 199 W. 8th Ave., Suite 3, Eugene, OR 97401.

Resource Publications
An Imprint of Wipf and Stock Publishers
199 W. 8th Ave., Suite 3
Eugene, OR 97401

www.wipfandstock.com

PAPERBACK ISBN: 978-1-5326-6431-1
HARDCOVER ISBN: 978-1-5326-6432-8
EBOOK ISBN: 978-1-5326-6433-5

Scripture quotations are from New Revised Standard Version Bible, copyright © 1989 National Council of the Church of Christ in the United States of America. Used by permission. All rights reserved worldwide.

Manufactured in the U.S.A.

Contents

Preface | vii
Acknowledgments | xv

Chapter 1 Thinking in Systems: An Historical Overview of Family Therapy | 1

Chapter 2 Toward a Theology of Hope: Speaking the Goodness of God in a Pathological Culture | 28

Chapter 3 The Magic of Language: Hope-Filled Conversations in Pastoral Care | 42

Chapter 4 The Basics of Solution-Focused Counseling | 49

Chapter 5 Protecting Those in Our Care: Ethical Guidelines for Lay Caregivers and the Church | 74

Final Words | 93
Conclusion | 99
Bibliography | 101

Preface

Zechariah chapter 8 provides an idyllic description of the streets of Jerusalem after God has returned the remnant and restored the city. Verses 4 and 5 announce, "Thus says the Lord of hosts: Old men and old women shall again sit in the streets of Jerusalem, each with staff in hand because of their great age. And the streets of the city shall be full of boys and girls playing in its streets."[1] I remember going to the mall several years ago with my mother and seeing her purse strapped over her shoulder. She clutched it defensively under her arm, afraid that someone might try to take it from her. My observation that day was that culture has reached an awful low when a kind old woman feels threatened in such a public place.

The next Sunday we went to church, and as we returned to the parking lot after the service, she realized that she had left her purse somewhere in the building. In this setting, rather than protectively tucking it under her arm, she had nonchalantly left it on the pew as she turned and greeted friends. Like the aged men and women in the New Jerusalem, she felt safe in this sacred place.

Children are also different in the picture from Zechariah, safely playing in the streets. When our children were small and we went out in public, I didn't take my eyes off of them for two minutes. I wanted to know where they were and that they were safe. But at church, things were different for them. I didn't have to

1. Zechariah 8:4–5, NRSV; this book will primarily use the NRSV translation of Scripture unless otherwise stated.

PREFACE

keep an eye on them because I knew and trusted that they were in the midst of friends. The church—the Kingdom of God on Earth—may not yet be perfect, but it is a community that offers peace, safety, and hope for our broken world.

This book is for that Kingdom. It offers leaders in the church a way of caring for and equipping one another that I believe can help us to more effectively be the body of Christ. I intentionally use the word "effectively" because I want to offer a practical, realistic, and unpretentious model for mobilizing members in the local congregation to care for one another in ways that can help us experience the joy, freedom, and safety that we will ultimately know in the New Jerusalem. I also use the word "effectively" with caution because I do not believe that programs or techniques are ultimately the keys to be the body of Christ. These are useful tools, but becoming the body of Christ is not a mechanistic process. It is a gift of God's grace and work in our lives.

The approach to caring for one another that I offer in this work is grounded in a model known as Solution-Focused Counseling. In the words of Howard Stone, Professor of Pastoral Theology and Pastoral Counseling at Brite Divinity School, and editor of the Fortress Press series *Creative Pastoral Care and Counseling*, Solution-Focused Counseling is the "best way to help our parishioners through their difficulties so that they can regain hope and be faithful to God's call."[2]

Solution-Focused theory offers a contrast to the predominantly deficit-based language of contemporary psychology and mental health. In the brokenness of this world, our culture and our churches have almost unequivocally accepted the dominant paradigm of a medical model of psychology that focuses on causal diagnosis and psychotropic treatment of every human problem, from sexual dysfunction to depression to inappropriate classroom behavior. Certainly, there are times when the medical approach to psychology is helpful. Members of my own family have benefited from the use of psychotherapeutic drugs. However, I believe that a wholesale acceptance of the medical model can and does often

2. Stone, "Congregational Setting of Pastoral Counseling," 189.

paralyze its users in a reliance on individualistic, dysfunctional, and deterministic frames of reference.

In his controversial book *The Myth of Mental Illness*, published in 1974, author Thomas Szasz exposes the weaknesses of the medical model, stating that we thus "remain shackled to the wrong conceptual framework and terminology," and, therefore, "the language of psychiatry (and psychoanalysis) is fundamentally unfaithful to its own subject."[3] Szasz goes on to propose that we need a language of psychology that will "reintroduce freedom, choice, and responsibility into the conceptual framework of psychiatry."[4] The assumptions and techniques of Solution-Focused theory are one example of this kind of alternative language. Particularly, students of this theory will discover that the introduction of freedom, choice, and responsibility is at the crux of the approach.

The fundamental purpose of this book is to guide ministers in equipping the members of their congregations to care for one another. Stone states, "When it comes to guiding people through life's difficulties and crises, America's clergy long have been—and still are—at the front lines."[5] In a 1994 study of frequent churchgoers, Gayle Privette, Stephen Quackenbos, and Charles M. Bundrick found these individuals seven times more likely to seek the assistance of clergy—rather than a counselor in the secular realm—during times of marital or family distress.[6] Moreover, Philip S. Wang, Patricia A. Berglund, and Ronald C. Kessler report that one quarter of those who have ever sought treatment for mental disorders did so from a clergy member, and that individuals continue to contact clergy for this type of help at higher proportions than both psychiatrists (16.7 percent) and general medical doctors (16.7 percent).[7]

---

3. Szasz, *Myth of Mental Illness*, 4–5.

4. Szasz, *Myth of Mental Illness*, 6.

5. Stone, "Congregational Setting of Pastoral Counseling," 181.

6. Privette et al., "Preferences for Religious and Nonreligious Counseling and Psychotherapy," 539.

7. Wang et al., "Patterns and Correlates of Contacting Clergy," 1.

PREFACE

Put simply, clergy members have a high level of responsibility. With this in mind, it is important to note that, according to the 2018 report "The State of Mental Health in America," published by Mental Health America, "1 of 5 Americans have a mental health condition," yet "56% of adults with a mental illness did not receive treatment."[8] These statistics make it clear that already overworked ministers cannot be expected to carry the weight of caregiving in our churches. A large percentage of people in genuine need of counsel are not being served.

Siang-Yang Tan, professor of psychology at Fuller Theological Seminary and senior pastor of First Evangelical Church in Glendale, California, observes that the shortage of mental health workers is one of the reasons why "lay counseling has become a significant part of the contemporary mental health scene."[9]

Tan and others have advocated the practice of lay counseling within the local church for a number of years.[10] Tan notes that paraprofessional training in basic counseling and helping skills usually includes "listening and empathy skills as well as referral skills but can also be broadened to include some cognitive-behavioral, marital and family, or systemic counseling methods."[11] I agree with Tan; we can equip lay counselors beyond the basics. From my own education in these additional skills, Solution-Focused Counseling offers the best and most practical concepts for additional training.

The reality is that ministers can't do it all on their own. Yet even more important than this fact are the biblical and theological injunctions that the community of Christ is called and privileged to "bear one another's burdens"[12] and to "provoke one another to love

---

8. "State of Mental Health in America," http://www.mentalhealthamerica.net/issues/state-mental-health-america.

9. Tan, *Lay Counseling*, 61; Crabb, *Effective Biblical Counseling*; Howe, *A Pastor in Every Pew*; Lampe, *The Caring Congregation*; and Stephen Ministries, https://www.stephenministries.org/default.cfm.

10. See for example: Tan, S. 1991. Crabb, Effective Biblical Counseling; Howe, A Pastor in Every Pew; Lampe, The Caring Congregation; and Stephen Ministries, https://www.stephenministries.org/default.cfm.

11. Tan, "Role of the Psychologist," 361.

12. Galatians 6:2.

and good deeds."[13] It is in caring for others and being cared for by others that we truly find the joy of living in God's community.

While there are a number of models and training programs for Christian lay counselors, to date there are no training manuals that equip the laity in the application of Solution-Focused approaches. One of the reasons why the Solution-Focused model has not found its way into the lay Christian counseling movement may be that the larger field of pastoral counseling is only recently beginning to accept the approach. As Stone comments, the pastoral counseling field is "developmentally stuck" in a "therapeutic model of an earlier era."[14] As a discussion of the theory will later explain, Solution-Focused Counseling works collaboratively with clients, rather than in the paternalistic styles of the past in which the counselor is the expert. Larry Crabb, a well-known author in the field of Christian Counseling, states that "the lay counseling movement has not challenged the basic thing I'm challenging, which is the expert-elder distinction. I think they still operate under the assumption that people need a specialist—an expert with certified training who has more than biblical wisdom, personal godliness and deep compassion."[15]

I have developed and tested the content of this book and the application of its ideas, both in classes on pastoral care that I regularly teach and in working with a number of churches over the years that were beginning ministries of lay caregiving. In several of these churches, the individuals who received training now carry the bulk of pastoral care in their congregations. These good people are living testimonies to the validity of this approach. In the words of one trainee, "I have confidence about what I am doing because of success in using the model in the past. I have tested the model, and, like practicing my golf swing, I know that it works."

Throughout this book, I rely on my own experiences counseling individuals and teaching others to counsel. It should be made

---

13. Hebrews 10:24.
14. Stone, "Congregational Setting of Pastoral Counseling," 187.
15. Crabb, *Basic Principles of Biblical Counseling*, 17.

clear that appropriate steps have been taken to protect client identity and confidentiality in all counseling conversations included in these pages.

Chapter 1 begins this book with an overview of the theoretical developments in the field of family therapy. I explain transitions in the assumptions about the role of the counselor in working with individuals and families, from (1) the early cybernetic systems perspectives to (2) cybernetics of cybernetics to (3) social construction. This historical framework is important because it demonstrates not just the developments in family therapy but also the mindset that made the developments toward Solution-Focused theory possible. The second chapter seeks to provide a theological treatment of the concept of Solution-Focused Counseling, proposing that the collaborative and hope-filled dynamics of this theory are consistent with sound practical theology. Chapter 3 introduces the more specific assumptions of the Solution-Focused model. These first chapters are more theoretical than pedagogic, presenting an essential discussion of the fundamental ideas that ground the approach. The intention of these discussions is to provide the reader with an adequate lens for thinking "Solution-Focused."

My experience in teaching curriculum that another author prepared is that adapting the material for presentation in my own voice is the first challenge. Solution-Focused theory is a unique frame of reference for thinking about the problems and difficulties of living. Rather than rote presentation of this material, I encourage you, the trainer, to freely adapt and adjust these ideas to your own voice. I believe that staying within the Solution-Focused perspective is a most important function in training others to apply the model, and I hope that the first three chapters will provide enough of that perspective that it can become your own. The Solution-Focused model assumes that past success can lead to success in the future; with this assumption in mind, I also encourage you to prepare by thinking of past instances when you have presented other material and to incorporate what you do well into these presentations. The assumptions of the theory thus become the framework for the training itself. In other words, this is a Solution-Focused approach to training Solution-Focused counselors.

Chapters 4 and 5 are intended to serve more as a training manual than as a textbook, offering exercises, teaching materials, and other content I have found useful for equipping others in this approach to counseling. In presenting these ideas, I attempt to offer them in a way that is flexible and useful. My trust is that presenters will borrow freely from this material, adapting it and personalizing it at will, taking what is helpful and omitting what is not. I offer suggested exercises, discussion questions, and other teaching methods as examples of what I have developed and often borrowed from others. I have organized the material in sequences I have found the most logical, but the ideas are by no means prescriptive. In adapting the material and planning presentations, I encourage users to ground their own preparation in a Solution-Focused context.

My intention in offering these materials is that this manual will be a resource for the training of lay caregivers. As such, I hope that it is a practical and mature demonstration of one way to do this training. I remember reading a training manual for a now-forgotten program of ministry in which many of the author's suggestions were trivial and obvious. In contrast, this manual will not tell the reader, "Make sure you have enough markers and butcher paper for each participant." I trust that readers of this work can decide for themselves when to take a "punch and cookie break." The task of training people to care for one another calls for serious and in-depth preparation. This is my attempt to contribute an answer to that call.

The ultimate hope of this effort is grounded in the promise of Isaiah 9:2–6:

> The people who walked in darkness
>   have seen a great light;
> those who lived in a land of deep darkness—
>   on them light has shined.
> You have multiplied the nation,
>   you have increased its joy;

> they rejoice before you
>> as with joy at the harvest,
>> as people exult when dividing plunder.
> For the yoke of their burden,
>> and the bar across their shoulders,
>> the rod of their oppressor,
>> you have broken as on the day of Midian.
> For all the boots of the tramping warriors
>> and all the garments rolled in blood
>> shall be burned as fuel for the fire.
> For a child has been born for us,
>> a son given to us;
> authority rests upon his shoulders;
>> and he is named
> Wonderful Counselor, Mighty God,
>> Everlasting Father, Prince of Peace.[16]

If you or your trainees feel anxiety about helping others, you can relax because of this reality: the position of Wonderful Counselor is already occupied. We do not have to be wonderful counselors. Rather, our vocation as caring Christians is to participate in conversations with the people in our care that bring them into the presence of the Wonderful Counselor. It is the prayer of this book that the recipients of our care and those whom we train to care for others come to know the hope and joy of trusting our lives to this Wonderful Christ.

---

16. Isaiah 9:2–6.

Acknowledgments

It is my good fortune to teach at Emmanuel Christian Seminary at Milligan College, where I have the opportunity to present the concepts of this book to students preparing for ministry. Teaching at Emmanuel has also introduced me to good friends of the school, who have invited me to teach members of their congregations and to present these materials in a variety of other settings. I am grateful to those students and other participants for all of their interaction. They have given me valuable feedback, and the creativity they've shown making the concepts their own has contributed to these pages in immeasurable ways.

I have also been blessed by the institution's generous sabbatical policy, where the idea for compiling the content of those presentations into a book first began to emerge. After a number of starts, interruptions, and revisions, I turned to Valerie Kocsis for help in bringing it all together. Without her meticulous review of the entire document, her always-helpful suggestions, and her work compiling it all into a final form, I would be left with only a confusing collection of random files. I am sincerely grateful for her good work.

1

Thinking in Systems

*An Historical Overview
of Family Therapy*

I WAS FAIRLY NEW and inexperienced as a counseling intern when I scheduled the appointment to meet with Tim. From the mother's initial phone call, I knew that he was an eighth-grade teenager who had been having trouble at school and was suspended for fighting. Tim claimed that he was being bullied and that the other boy started the fight, and his mother believed him. His suspension from school would remain until he had completed seven sessions of Anger Management counseling, so she felt they had no option but to attend.

The first session began with Tim, his mother, and his younger sister in the room. His mother and sister sat next to each other on the small couch as Tim, ignoring my greeting, went to a chair in the corner. The mother began, expressing apologies for her husband's absence. At the last minute, he had informed her he had something at work to take care of, but that he would support anything I advised for their son. She added, "He agrees with the school that Tim has a problem with his anger and that I let him manipulate me by always taking his side."

By the end of our first session, I was asking if I really wanted to continue my preparation for ministry and pastoral care.

As I was leaving my office later that week, the phone rang. Tim's father was on the line asking if I could meet right away with him and his wife. When they arrived a few minutes later, Tim's mother had obviously been crying, and his father was distraught. Taking a seat on the couch and holding each other for emotional support, the father reported that Tim had been in another fight when he was not supposed to be on school property. Tim told his sister that he was sick of this family and was going to stay at a friend's house. My initial response was to ask about injuries and to confirm that both Tim and the other young man were safe. The father had called the school principal, who said that they "were not going to pursue the matter because it was not reported or witnessed, and no one was hurt." He then added, "This is Tim's last chance with me."

Tim's mother said, "We are at the end of our rope." Burying his face in his hands, the father said, "I am losing hope for my son."

Clearly this family was not functioning well, and one could certainly propose a number of interpretations for their condition. Interestingly, the neighbors who knew Tim's family often observed that on the occasions when Tim was in their homes, he was a normal, fun-loving young man.

In the view of Tim's father, however, Tim was the exact opposite of his younger sister, who could do no wrong. Perhaps the school officials were correct: "Tim had an anger management problem." Some might suggest that the father was distant and that his son was seeking attention. Or perhaps Tim's mother was overly responsible for her son and reinforced his attention-seeking behavior. If we asked her how she viewed these events, she might have said that she was just trying to be a good mother and that the only time her husband became involved was when Tim created some sort of crisis. The father, in response, might counter that Tim needed to learn that behavior has consequences, but that as long as she babied him, he was not likely to learn. A child psychologist might interpret the son's behavior as the beginning stages of an oppositional defiant disorder, or as the early onset of passive aggressive acting out. Perhaps, if asked why he was behaving in this way, Tim would have answered like most teenagers, with the familiar "I don't know."

In the same way, one could give a number of recommendations for these parents to more successfully manage their troubled teen. Some might say that the parents needed to be firm, to practice tough love, and to quit letting their son manipulate them. Others might suggest that Tim had a psychological problem that needed to be addressed in ongoing therapy. A child psychologist might diagnose the onset of a behavioral disorder and prescribe a variety of mood-altering medications along with a therapeutic treatment plan focused on managing his behavior. Cognitive theoretical approaches would seek to help Tim think differently about how he chose to behave.

I propose that the actual "why" of this situation—as well as any approach to helping the family—will ultimately arise from subjective assertions based on one's assumptions about human behavior and one's social location in this given situation. From this assertion, I believe that even the child psychologist, who might claim professional objectivity, would still operate from a particular set of assumptions that would be affirmed in a diagnosis. The notion that one right analysis is possible is a fallacy that fails to attend to the complicated nature of human relationships.

Thinking in Systems I: Cybernetics

For the purpose of this discussion, I offer another set of assumptions that can be enlightening in understanding family and group dynamics. The assumptions I propose are no less subjective than other possible explanations. I have biases shaped by the experiences of my own family dynamics, my education, and my location in the world. However, what follows also offers a different perspective, which focuses not on diagnosis but on moving toward an understanding of the dynamics at work in the relationships of the family members.

These assumptions are grounded in a systemic view of human interaction rooted in the theory of cybernetics. The term "cybernetics" comes from the Greek term for "governor," and the word is associated with the idea of a boat pilot, who must keep the boat in balance to stay on course. I will explain this metaphor further in a moment.

In the 1950s, the staff of a large mental hospital was engaged in a series of observations of patients being treated for Schizophrenia. The researchers noticed that when family members visited, the symptomatic behavior of their patients often escalated. Further observation led them to hypothesize that communication in these families often took place on two levels, which they identified as conflicting verbal and non-verbal messages. For example, they noted that in the initial greetings of these family members, the parents extended "warm greetings followed by stiffening physical postures when they hugged their child." These observations led the team to focus on the "interactional" patterns of the families, in contrast to their previous focus on the individual behaviors and mental states of the patients.[1]

This is an admittedly brief description of a long course of events and research; however, it summarizes what, for some in the field of psychology, represents a monumental epistemological shift. Put simply, this breakthrough introduced a revolutionary approach to understanding and treating mental illness and human behavior. For these researchers and others who adopted their insights, this perspective introduced a change from the traditional linear, cause-and-effect explanations of dysfunction to a non-linear, recursive, process-oriented frame of reference. As will be delineated in subsequent discussions, this epistemological shift has continued and is still evolving in ways that are substantially different from these earliest developments. These later discussions will demonstrate that the field of family therapy has transitioned through three major stages characterized as 1) Cybernetics, 2) Cybernetics of Cybernetics, and 3) Social Construction. Throughout this transformation, family therapists have often positioned themselves at the cutting-edge of mental health care. A review of these three theoretical transitions will be helpful in building a foundation for actually applying these perspectives in a counseling relationship.

1. Bateson et al., "Toward a Theory of Schizophrenia," 217.

One of the most theoretically prolific authors in the literature on cybernetics is Gregory Bateson, who observed that human interaction with other living things takes place on a different logical level than human interaction with the non-living. Bateson illustrated his point by observing that when a man kicks a pebble, the pebble rolls as a result of the energy produced by the foot, until the energy is spent. According to Bateson, if the man kicks a dog, the transfer of energy will have a larger repertoire of possible outcomes beyond merely rolling until the energy of the kick expires. This is because, unlike the inanimate pebble, the dog has the capacity to react. This difference is based on the fact that at some level, the dog perceives the kick as "communication." Also, at some level, the dog perceives relationship, has some sort of self-understanding, and possesses some level of emotion. The dog may run away, may attack, or may react in any number of ways, all depending on innumerable factors including the dog's basic nature, prior history of being kicked, relationship with the man, and so on.[2] Bateson and others have proposed that this higher logical level of interaction between living things can be examined within the principles of cybernetic—or systemic—patterns.

This systemic paradigm asks many different questions about the processes of interaction and is not concerned with typical cause-and-effect explanations. The causal-oriented question "Why?" may explain that the pebble rolled because the man kicked it. In answer to the question "Why did the dog run away?" however, the answer "Because the man kicked it" is unsatisfactory because relational variables are possible between a man and a dog that are not possible between a man and a rock. Did the dog growl at the man who, fearing that he was about to be bitten, chose to strike first? If so, perhaps the man first threatened the dog by coming into the dog's fenced yard. Clearly, a variety of sequences of events might be possible that, as in the earlier example of the teenage son and his parents, are subjectively interpreted. Systems theory offers a number of unique principles that are useful for examining these relational interactions.

2. Bateson, *Ecology of Mind*, 489–90.

The Assumptions of Family Systems

To introduce these principles, it is helpful to begin with a common illustration of systemic function. Think of a thermostat in a heating and cooling system. If the thermostat is set at seventy degrees, this temperature is not a static measure of the temperature in the room; rather, it is the middle point of a range of temperatures that may extend from, say, sixty-eight to seventy-two degrees. If it is warmer than seventy-two degrees outside of the cooling and heating system's environment when the thermostat is set to seventy degrees, the air conditioner will begin to cool the room. Cool air will continue to circulate from the air conditioner until sixty-eight degrees—the low end of the temperature range—is reached. Sensing that it has reached this limit, the thermostat sends a message to the air conditioner to stop blowing cool air. With air no longer blowing, the room temperature will begin to rise until it reaches the upper limit of seventy-two degrees, at which point the thermostat will send the message to the air conditioner to reactivate and begin cooling the room. This interaction is circular, or recursive, repeating and self-correcting around the seventy-degree setting.

From this illustration, we can begin to delineate some of the basic principles of cybernetic systems:

Nonsummativity

This principle stresses the perspective that the system in its entirety is more than just the sum of its parts. A dismantled air conditioner, with parts spread across the technician's worktable, is not an air conditioning system. Only when the parts are functioning together are they a system.

Wholeness

Based on the idea of nonsummativity, the concept of wholeness explains that change in one member of the system can influence the whole system. For example, if a blade in the fan that blows cool air breaks down, the whole system is changed.

Homeostasis

Homeostasis refers to the equilibrium of the system in which the upper and lower limits of behavior are regulated. The boundaries in the heating and cooling system of seventy-two and sixty-eight degrees sustain the behavior of the system.

Stochastic Process

With the ability to store information for future use, certain patterns may become repetitive and more probable than others. In the heating and cooling system, we can predict that unless there is some systemic abnormality, the range of temperature will continue within the set boundaries.

Feedback

All systems contain either negative or positive feedback. Negative feedback is that which reduces deviation, and positive feedback amplifies deviation. In this instance, the cooling and heating system is a negative feedback system. Students who are new to systems theory will do well to recognize that negative feedback is an amoral concept. Rather than a common understanding of negative as bad and positive as good, negative merely means that the system is constant in its fluctuation. Depending on the systemic patterns and one's perspective, this can be either "good" or "bad." A healthy system, as in a functioning cooling and heating system, is characterized by its negative feedback. In this example, positive feedback—such as a broken fan blade—produces deviation in the healthy system.

Punctuation

This principle observes that in a systemic process, the concept of a starting point is a linear and subjective notion that fails to account for the recursive patterns of the system. The heating and cooling system does not have a literal starting point. The importance of this principle in relational systems can be seen in the human proclivity to assign blame. In the story of Tim's family at the beginning of the chapter, the mother might say that the process begins with the father's absenteeism, while the father might alternately claim that it is the result of her being overbearing.

Communications Theory and Cybernetics

A clear and practical understanding of the application of cybernetic systems theory in human relationship functioning also relies on principles from communications theory. Following this brief delineation of communication principles, I will propose a cybernetic description of this family.

Complementary/Symmetrical

These two constructs demonstrate an important framework for viewing the dynamic patterns of relationship systems. Understanding their function together depends on first understanding the nature of each.

Complementary patterns are patterns that are different but fit together. An illustration of a complementary pattern is the relationship between a quarterback and a receiver. Both have a different function but need each other to complete their combined purpose of moving the football down the field. In similar fashion, a violin and a bow are complementary, having different functions but needing each other to produce their sound. In human relationships, examples of complementary patterns can include dominance/submission, leading/following, arguing/complying, and so on.

Symmetrical patterns, in contrast, fit together because they match. An example of a symmetrical pattern is the relationship in a game of tennis. While the tennis racket and ball are complementary, the tennis racket of one opponent and the racket of another are symmetrical, serving the same function. The nuclear arms race is a symmetrical pattern; as country A builds its arsenal, country

B matches the behavior by building its own arsenal. In contrast, a complementary move by either country would be to de-escalate the pattern in some sort of peace-making expression—that is to say, threatening war/asking for peace would be complementary. Other examples of symmetrical relationship patterns might include arguing/arguing, crying/crying, teasing/teasing, and so on.

We can observe the dynamic function of these two principles in the theory of cybernetic systems. In essence, the relationship between symmetrical and complementary patterns demonstrates the concept of homeostasis. Returning to the heating and cooling system, one can see that the mechanisms maintaining the negative feedback of the room temperature alternate between symmetrical (or matching) and complementary (or different) as the temperature fluctuates between its upper and lower homeostatic boundaries. When the system, in a symmetrical (matching) mode of cooling/cooling, reaches the bottom level of homeostasis at sixty-eight degrees, it recalibrates itself and becomes complementary (different) until the upper level of homeostasis at seventy-two degrees is reached. Clearly the system is not static, as it alternates between these symmetrical and complementary patterns.

Similar symmetrical/complementary patterns are common in human relationships—between most spouses, for instance. I have observed this at times in my own marriage. Perhaps my wife and I have a disagreement, and we each begin to argue our side of the issue. The argument proceeds in a symmetrical pattern; we express our strong opinions back and forth, back and forth, even matching each other in the rising tone of our voices. At some point, the argument reaches a point where the pattern shifts and becomes complementary. Perhaps one of our children enters the room, or one of us says, "We need to stop before one of us says something we don't mean." There are countless ways for the system to reverse itself, and from a systems perspective, it always will unless there is real secondary change.

Digital/Analogic

Communications theory also recognizes that communication involves much more than mere words; it includes non-verbal behavior as well. Making eye contact, looking away, smiling, frowning, or rolling the eyes can all be classified as communication. A passenger taking a seat on a plane, immediately putting in earphones, and beginning to read a book is communicating a message to the person in the next seat: "I don't want to talk." Not speaking to someone sends a powerful message that, even without words, is a communication. The point is that behavior communicates. Even misbehaving is still "behaving" because there is no opposite of behavior. So, in communications theory, we don't just deal with words. We consider behavior with the strong assumption that behavior communicates, and (pardon the double negative) "you cannot, not communicate.[3]" As will be explained later, the importance of this perspective in systems theory is that a relationship system behaves in systemic fashion.

These two modes of communicating—verbal and non-verbal—are conceptualized in linguistics as digital and analogic communication, respectively. Put simply, digital communication contains the actual words of the message, while analogic communication holds the meaning that is intended in the message. Another term that is sometimes used to describe analogic communication is "performative." Putting on earphones and reading a book is an analogic, performative, non-verbal message. The digital version of the same communication would be something like, "Don't talk to me; I want to be left alone to read my book." One could probably conclude that, at least in this instance, analogical communication is preferred over digital because verbally communicating the message "don't talk to me" would appear rude. The problem with analogic communication is that it lacks the explanatory qualities of digital communication, so that in this instance, telling a neighboring passenger, "I would prefer not to visit," probably has a better

---

3. Watzlawick et al., *Pragmatics of Human Communication*, 32.

chance of communicating clearly than putting on earphones and hoping the other person gets the message.

Most misunderstandings in human relationships occur at the analogic level. While someone might misunderstand the words used in a digital communication, the listener can ask for clarification. Analogic communication, on the other hand, tends to be more ambiguous and, without a digital clarification, subject to false interpretation. For example, if someone is crying, there is no way from a purely analogic frame to interpret whether the tears are tears of sorrow or of joy. With further information from the context of what is going on, an interpretation is more likely. One can probably safely infer that tears at a funeral home are different from tears in a labor and delivery room, but ultimately, analogic messages usually need some explanatory, digital clarification.

Anyone who has ever taken a lie detector test could confirm the fact that communicating a message involves not just words but also the unspoken anxiety that the polygraph measures. Is the digital meaning of growing pale, trembling, sweating, and stammering an indication of guilt, or is it the fear of being found guilty although innocent? This dynamic is also clearly at work in the courtroom because our legal system is based almost entirely on digital communication, and analogic interpretation is treated as hearsay.

On the other hand, it is important to note that analogic communication is often more effective in communicating the emotions of a relationship than digital communication. In most instances, a warm hug in the right context is more meaningful than the mere digital phrase, "I care about you." Modern technology has tried to find a way through this ambiguity. When an email is sent, the computer tries to incorporate an analogic explanation for the digital message by giving the speaker the option of placing an emoticon at the end of a sentence, but even emoticons are ultimately digital messages because, like words, they are agreed-upon symbols that are intended to mean something.

Report/Command

Communications theory also recognizes that most messages contain a report aspect and a command aspect. The report aspect of a communication is simply the information in the message, while the command aspect contains the expectation of how the message is to be understood. A message that is meant as sarcasm has a different command than a message that is meant sincerely. Misunderstandings about the command aspect of a message are also common reasons for relationship disagreements. As an example, consider the report (i.e., the information) in the statement, "The garbage is piling up." The command aspect of this information (i.e., how it is to be understood) is complicated by simply considering its context. The statement, "The garbage is piling up" uttered by the owner of a landfill probably has a different command than if the statement comes from a mother speaking to her fourteen-year-old son as she stands at the door of his bedroom. While the statement made at the landfill might be an observation about how good business is, the mother's statement is probably an encouragement for her son to clean the room.

The Relational Aspect of Communicating Behavior

A related presupposition to the above principles recognizes that communicating behavior is relational. The mother's message to the son about the trash piling up is most likely a request to clean things up. The message of putting on earphones and reading says, "I would prefer not to visit," and it also says, "I see you, the passenger next to me, as a potential interruption of that preference." So, in essence, communicating behavior says, "This is how I see you seeing me, and this is how I want you to see me." In the airplane relationship, one may communicate back to the other by confirming her desire; not trying to engage the other in conversation at some level says, "I see you seeing me as someone who might try to disrupt your privacy, but I don't intend to speak either," so the first passenger puts on his earphones, too. Or he may communicate back to his neighbor, "I see you as a snob who needs to be challenged to learn to be friendly," so he taps his seat partner on the knee and asks, "What are you reading?" In the same way, the son may roll his eyes at the mother's observation about the garbage, again a communicating response that contains how he sees her, and how he wants to be seen. The craziness of this whole principle is that the this-is-how-I-see-you-seeing-me interaction is theoretically infinitely recursive: "This is how I see you seeing me, see you, seeing me . . ." *ad infinitum.*

More will be said about this later, but one of the important implications of this idea is that when traditional psychology speaks of constructs as solitary abstractions that are somehow contained within the individual's mind, it fails to acknowledge the relational aspect of behavior. Paul Watzlawick explains:

> When the vocabulary of experimental psychology was extended to interpersonal contexts, the language of psychology still remained a monadic one. Concepts such as leadership, dependency, extroversion and introversion, nurturance and many others if only thought and repeated long enough, assume a pseudo-reality of their own, and eventually "leadership" the construct becomes Leadership, a measurable quantity in the human mind, conceived as a phenomenon in isolation. Once this reification has taken place, it is no longer recognized that the term is but a shorthand expression for a particular form of ongoing relationship.[4]

In other words, we don't really understand leadership as a distinct property; we understand leadership as a particular style of relating to another style of relating—in this case, following. Thus, leadership describes a complementary relationship with following. Gregory Bateson gives a similar perspective, noting that "[p]sychologists commonly speak as if the abstractions of relationships (dependency, hostility, love, etc.) were real things which are to be described or expressed by messages. This is epistemology backwards: in truth, the messages (or behaviors)

---

4. Watzlawick et al., *Pragmatics of Human Communication*, 7–8.

constitute the relationship, and words like dependency are verbally coded descriptions of patterns immanent in the combination of exchanged messages."[5]

In communications theory, terms like passive aggression, depression, and co-dependency are all descriptions of relationship patterns, rather than internal entities, because they all imply the sending of a this-is-me-seeing-you-seeing-me message. Anyone who has ever attempted to talk someone out of being depressed knows that efforts to be encouraging and hopeful are often met with greater despair, so we try harder to be positive, which often reinforces the person's demonstration of depression. It is an endless pattern that is illustrated by one of the golden maxims of marriage and family therapy: "If you always do what you've always done, you'll always get what you always got."

A Systemic View of Relationships

This chapter began with a description of Tim, a teenage son and his struggling parents. I observed that one could propose a variety of analyses for understanding this family's difficulties. Additionally, I observed that rather than one right diagnosis being possible, any prescription for this family's condition would be grounded in the particular assumptions of the diagnostician. A cause-and-effect rationale (commonly assumed by the general public, as well as the field of traditional psychology, to be the most logical approach) would most likely assess the family members with individualistic, linear-based conclusions. A systemic perspective, on the other hand, engenders a different possibility. In the analysis that follows, I will apply the various systemic principles that have been delineated to the case of Tim and his family, and I will conclude with an overall systemic perspective on the family.

---

5. Bateson, *Ecology of Mind*, 275.

Nonsummativity

To review, the principle of nonsummativity recognizes that the individual members of a system do not equal the system. In the case of this teenage son, his misbehaving behavior occurred within the systemic patterns of his family. Other parents did not experience the misbehaving when he was in their homes. Tim's (mis)behavior—and that of his family members—was clearly taking place within the boundaries of the family relationships. Thus, the family system was more than the sum of its parts.

Wholeness

The idea of wholeness is more aptly applied to an assumption of treatment that believes a change in one member of the system can influence the entire system. This change can also be understood as positive feedback. In the patterns of this family, a change that would influence the whole system might be the sudden illness of one of the parents, or some other event that would alter their typical style of relating. While it would be tragic, the development of the illness causing a change in the system would be, by definition, classified as positive feedback.

Homeostasis

Recall that this concept entails the upper and lower boundaries of the system that behaves within a prescribed range. The modulation of the heating and cooling system between the two extreme temperatures illustrates the homeostatic concept. Another frequently used illustration is to think of two passengers standing side-by-side on a small boat. If passenger A leans over the side of the boat, threatening to capsize the vessel, passenger B self-protectively and logically leans to the other side of the boat to bring it into balance. In similar fashion, relationship systems modulate between two extremes. As in the case of the boat passengers, it is most helpful in perceiving the function of a system to observe the behaviors of the system's members at their extreme positions.

The homeostasis of Tim's family was characterized by the extreme behaviors of each member. At one extreme, the mother felt completely responsible for the son, while at the other extreme, the father removed himself from the interaction. In the same way, the son acted out in a way that involved both parents, while the younger sister stood in contrast as the model child. In my own experience with counseling, families often reach out for counseling help when the extreme behaviors are either threatening to or have exceeded the homeostatic boundaries to which the families have become accustomed.

Stochastic Process

The pattern of leaning to an opposite extreme to maintain balance is a stochastic process in that the behaviors of the system reinforce the other behaviors. This makes the pattern more likely to continue. When passenger A leans to one side, passenger B leans to the other. A will continue leaning, which will reinforce B's leaning, which will reinforce A's, *ad infinitum*. In the case of Tim's family, the father is often perceived as absent, so the mother becomes more responsible, which in turn reinforces the father's absence. Clearly, as the patterns in this family developed, they simultaneously became more likely over time.

Feedback

The above description of the boat demonstrates a negative feedback system in that each member of the system behaves to reinforce or maintain the pattern of the system. Positive feedback would be the introduction of a behavior that alters this systemic pattern. If a shark began to circle the boat, the leaning-out behavior of the passengers would probably change. The negative feedback in the boat is performed by each member's extreme behavior. In the same way, the extreme behaviors in Tim's family describe an ongoing pattern of reinforcing the other extremes.

Punctuation

The punctuation of this system is most clearly understood in the variety of opinions that each person had about who was at fault. The mother felt that she was being the good parent and that the father was uninvolved; the father thought he was being the good parent because the mother was overbearing. They did not see that their individual extremes were both contributing to reinforce the son's behavior.

Complementary/Symmetrical

One application of this communication dynamic can be seen in the over-involved/under-involved complementary pattern of the mother and father. This pattern became symmetrical in my office when the parents were united in their distress about their troubled son.

Digital/Analogic

A good illustration of how digital and analogic communication can sometimes be contradictory—and thus reinforce relationship patterns—was evident in the father's disparate communications. His digital communication emphasized his support for the counseling process, but the analogic message of his absence at the first session contradicted this.

Report/Command

The mother apologized for her husband's absence and also related his belief that she routinely allowed Tim to manipulate her. While her statement reported the husband's actual words, the meaning (or command) that she intended seemed to be disagreement.

The Relational Aspect of Communicating Behavior

By now it should be obvious that behavior communicates. In this family, "This is how I see you seeing me" often resulted in contradictory messages, such as the mother's desire to be seen as both firm and maternally available. In a similar fashion, the father's communication of not engaging his son or wife was an analogic communication that he disagreed with how she was managing Tim. Her interpretation of that behavior was that the father was disengaged and expected her to manage Tim.

An overall systemic description of this family can begin by noticing how the extreme behaviors in the system reinforced the opposite extreme (providing negative feedback) in a way that balanced the system. Remembering that the principle of punctuation means that we can begin at any point in the circular pattern, this description will begin with the behavior of the father. His extreme position of non-involvement reinforced the mother's over-involvement. The son's extreme behavior of doing things that aggravated or worried his parents reinforced their complementary positions of non-involvement/over-involvement. The younger sister's pattern of being the ideal child reinforced the complementary behavior of her brother as the bad son.

As mentioned earlier, this pattern is not a static mechanism. Complementary and symmetrical relationships reverse at the upper or lower homeostatic boundary. In this instance, the complementary non-involved/over-involved pattern of the mother and father switched to a symmetrical relationship of concern/concern when the son's misbehavior reached the boundary extreme and he triggered their joint concern at the crisis of his last fight. A similar triggering response at the opposite extreme of concern/concern was the parents' agreement that they had done all they could and would no longer rescue him. Notice in this pattern that try harder/give up is a complementary dynamic.

In conclusion, we can observe that the various behaviors in this family fit together in such a way that they reinforce each other. These negative feedback patterns demonstrate a more-of-the-same, *ad infinitum* system, characterized by trying harder what is already not working in the family members' attempts to solve their problem.

This interpretation of the family patterns may seem to portray them as bad parents, or as a dysfunctional family. Reaching that conclusion is, I believe, contrary to the perspective offered by the model of care that will be presented in the coming chapters. In my interactions with the family, I came to know them as individuals who were each doing what they thought best for their family and for themselves. They loved and cared deeply for each other. They were not bad people. In their frustrations over the patterns taking place between them, they continued—as we are all prone to do—to try harder what had already not worked, and what was unfortunately reinforcing the difficult experiences in their lives.

So, what is a counselor or pastor to do when called on for help like this? As the counselor sitting with the distraught parents, worn out and frustrated by what they view as their problem child, what can I possibly say or do that will help this family? To begin to formulate a response that deals with these systemic patterns requires a theoretical move to the second part of this chapter: cybernetics of cybernetics.

Thinking in Systems II: Cybernetics of Cybernetics

In their despair, anxiety, and utter frustration with their son's behavior, these parents called on me to help. Sitting across from them brought an overwhelming feeling of responsibility. Without being totally aware of these systemic dynamics, I was invited into the private intricacies of their family relationships. I had a relationship with each member of this group. I was informed of their various viewpoints. I was asked to lend my help. In short, I was now a member of the system.

In the earliest stages of systemic theories of family therapy, the counselor or therapist was seen as an expert existing outside of the system. In the illustration of cybernetics functioning as a heating/cooling system, an expert mechanic would diagnose any problem within the system and make the necessary repairs. Early family therapy operated from the same principle: the professional was outside the system, and with the tools of his training, he applied a unique expertise designed to fix the broken family. What this example fails to identify is that the very presence of the expert impacts the system and, in essence, creates a new system. In the heating/cooling system, the mere physical presence of the mechanic—including body temperature, specific training and experience, and countless other factors—shapes his interaction with the system.

The same can be said of family systems. The expert brings her training, experience with families, personality, likes and dislikes, and so on to the family system. The family systems in which we grew up often have an extremely powerful impact on how we react to the families in our care, particularly when we have failed to resolve issues with our families of origin. A counselor who grew up with a distant and uninvolved father would probably have a different reaction to Tim's family than if he grew up with an overbearing father. Knowing ourselves and exploring our own families of origin can be an important element in learning how to manage the reactions that we have to the families we serve.

A great privilege—and responsibility—of our entrée as experts into family systems is that our presence is an instance of positive feedback. In other words, something outside of the calibrated system is engaged. In that regard, the counselor's ability to participate as a healthy member of the system is of paramount importance. This was a crucial step in the evolution of family systems theory: the recognition that the counselor was not a passive expert who observed, diagnosed, and acted from outside the system. Rather, the counselor was joining the system—and thus creating a *new* system. This realization came to be known as "cybernetics of cybernetics."

While this insight may seem obvious to those with a postmodern frame of reference, it should be noted that this recognition occurred in an age of paternalistic approaches to mental health care. The professionally trained counselor was expected to have knowledge and expertise from which to enact a remedy that would fix the broken family members. In contrast, the non-traditional and revolutionary openness of the early researchers and practitioners of family therapy occurred within a milieu in which learning from the patient was a fundamental premise.[6]

This openness to learning from the subjects of care themselves, and the willingness to claim its own lack of objective knowledge, shaped the field of family therapy into a fertile soil for a subsequent realization that identified with the postmodern theory of social construction.

The reader may notice that this discussion around cybernetics of cybernetics was rather brief compared to the earlier discussion of cybernetic systems. In a sense, this brevity illustrates the rapid transition from (1) cybernetics to (2) cybernetics of cybernetics to (3) social construction. To explain this rapid transition, two observations may be instructive. First, the transition from cybernetics of cybernetics to social construction came at a time of heightened sensitivity to the fallacy of objective knowledge; in this theoretical context, it was a logical next step. As will be discussed, the fallacy of objectivity is a fundamental tenet of social construction. Second, although it is helpful to delineate the three phases theoretically, it is important to note that in their practical applications to counseling, the transitions have developed in a less progressive fashion. While these developments are not as linear as the following table might suggest, it may still help the reader to compare the developments of these three phases.

---

6. For an engaging and thought-provoking discussion of how modern psychology and its language shaped its own authoritative position in Western culture, the interested reader may wish to consult Illouz, *Saving the Modern Soul*.

Cybernetics "Observed Systems"	Cybernetics of Cybernetics "Observing Systems"	Social Construction "Language Systems"
Therapist as expert	Therapist as member of the system	Therapist as not-knowing
Strategic Family Therapy	Radical Constructivism	Problem-Defined Systems
Structural Family Therapy	Reflective Therapy	Narrative Therapy
Bowen Family Therapy		Solution-Focused Counseling

Thinking in Systems III: Social Construction and the Postmodern Turn

Most serious presentations on postmodernism begin with the admission of how complicated and varied any attempt to nail down a precise understanding of the term really is. In seeking to make the following applicable to the actual practice of counseling, I will ground this discussion in the field of linguistics. By examining how language structures our world, we enter into the study of epistemology, or rather a way of recognizing how people come to construct and maintain their understandings of the world. At its most basic level, that's what postmodernism is about; it is a description of how people come to understand the world.

Postmodernism emphasizes that what one sees will always be shaped by the world in which one is presently operating. *How* one knows is inseparable from *what* one knows. As Alfred Korzybski famously noted, words are not maps of reality; rather, words gain their meaning through their use in social interchange within the language practice of the culture.[7] Korzybski goes on to explain that human beings often confuse what they think they know—the map—with

7. Korzybski, *Science and Sanity*, 750–51.

reality—the road. A typical illustration of this concept is that one does not sit down at a restaurant and eat the menu; the words that *describe* the food are certainly not the food themselves.

In human relationships, we often confuse our knowledge (our perceptions, interpretations, and so on) as the map or reality of what we experience. We don't use words like "perception," "thought," and "memory" because they accurately map out the world we call the mind. Rather, such terms gain their meaning from the way they are used in social interaction. To say to someone, "You forgot my birthday" is not a report on the state of the mental world; these are merely words that describe what one perceives as an error in the other's behavior.[8]

Clearly, in the example of the family with the misbehaving son, there were many interpretations or perceptions being employed by the various family members to diagnose the problem. Many perceptions are always possible. However, of one thing we can be certain: particularly when they are in the throes of emotionally and relationally intense difficulties, individuals will always construct some sort of interpretation, diagnosis, or explanation of every problem. As articulated by philosopher and professor of psychology Ernst von Glasersfeld, this search for an explanatory construct is often quite earnest:

> A key fits if it opens the lock. The fit describes a capacity of the key, not of the lock. Thanks to professional burglars we know only too well that there are many keys that are shaped quite differently from our own but which nevertheless unlock our doors. From the radical constructivist point of view, all of us—scientists, philosophers, laymen, school children, animals, and indeed, any kind of living organism—face our environment as a burglar faces a lock that he has to unlock in order to get at the loot.[9]

---

8. See earlier section: The Relational Aspect of Communicating Behavior.
9. Glasersfeld, *Radical Constructivism*, 21.

The Assumptions of Social Construction

The major tenets of social construction theory suggest that therapy is a linguistic event that takes place in conversation.[10] This theory proposes that problems and their solutions occur in the activity of conversation. With this major principle in mind, the counselor's primary task becomes one of managing the conversation in ways that help to change or solve the problem. Below, I will outline some additional assumptions of social construction theory that are important to this enterprise.

Realities Are Maintained by Social Interaction

This is a recursive concept in which those involved in the problem bring their interpretations to the conversation. As stated earlier, all behavior communicates, so this does not always imply speaking. To illustrate, think of the father's absence from the first counseling session. His distant behavior, perhaps based on his interpretation that the mother was being overbearing, reinforced her interpretation of his behavior as uncaring. Thus, she felt mandated to take full responsibility for Tim's behavior, which the father viewed as her being overbearing, which reinforced his distance . . . *ad infinitum.*

This type of interaction demonstrates well how an interpretation in turn confirms the language-originated realities.[11] Eugene S. Epstein and Victor E. Loos add, "The act of 'naming' objects or behavior (making distinctions) creates the reality experienced by the observer. Thus, the meanings around which people coordinate their behaviors are essentially a linguistic construction."[12] Laura Fruggeri suggests that these "language systems" operate as a hermeneutic circle of interaction in that beliefs held by individuals construct realities.[13] These realities are maintained by social interaction, which, in turn, confirms the beliefs that are socially originated.

10. Anderson and Goolishian, "Beyond Cybernetics," 157–63.
11. Hoffman, "Reflexive Stance," 4–17.
12. Epstein and Loos, "Some Irreverent Thoughts," 409.
13. Fruggeri, "Therapeutic Process," 43.

Problems Are Socially Constructed

Lynn Hoffman describes social construction theory as seeing "ideas, concepts and memories arising from social interchange and mediated through language."[14] From this perspective, problems are socially constructed realities as well and are also seen as occurring in language. As Jill Freedman and Gene Combs explain, "Problems develop when people internalize conversations that restrain them to a narrow description of self. These stories are experienced as oppressive because they limit the perception of available choices."[15] As with Tim's family, the ways they were talking were defining the problem.

Problems Define Systems

Following the idea that problems are socially constructed, a subsequent principle recognizes that, in contrast to earlier cybernetic theory, systems do not produce problems. From a paternalistic frame of reference, the cybernetic diagnostician assumed that systems had problems that could be expertly identified. As stated earlier, the cybernetic therapist understood herself as outside the system, enacting techniques of expertise to repair the broken system. In contrast, a social constructionist view, which assumes that problems are linguistic events, attends to the realities of participants in the problem. In this regard, participants in the problem are assumed to be those who are involved in communicating (and, therefore, behaving) about the problem. To illustrate, a collection of individuals—Tim, his mother, his father, his sister, the counselor, the school officials, the neighbors, and so on—comprised this specific problem-determined system.

Within the problem-determined system, praxis implications for the role of the counselor center on the counselor's use of self as a member of the system and on the importance of continuing the

---

14. Hoffman, "Reflexive Stance," 8.
15. Freedman and Combs, *Narrative Therapy*, 48.

conversation. In an approach known as "Multiple Engagement,"[16] Terry Real places the counselor in an interactive stance with each member of the system. In this engagement, the counseling conversation is seen as a continuous dialogue, which works toward creating new meanings that eventually "dis-solve" the problem.[17] Epstein and Loos add that "the goal of treatment, quite simply, is to maintain a conversation until what was originally defined as a problem is no longer viewed as a problem."[18]

To this discussion, Karen E. Kudlac brings a spiritual element, along with her agreement that participants in the therapeutic conversation are members of the problem-determined system. As was explained, membership in the system is defined as those who are involved in the problem conversation. We are also well aware that many individuals and families maintain a personal relationship with God and frequently turn to God in times of trouble. It is Kudlac's thesis that God, as a resource to the individual and the family, is also a member of the problem-determined system and should be included in the conversation.[19] The theological implications of this concept for pastoral caregivers deserve serious consideration regarding our own relationships with God, our beliefs and understandings about who God is, and how we represent God's work in people's lives.

Solutions Are Socially Constructed

If problems are created in language, then it follows that solutions and healing can be "brought forth" in conversation as well.[20] In this assumption, we find the fundamental perspective for those involved in creating healing conversations in this broken world. As those called to care, we are invited by those beset by the problems of their lives into the linguistic systems of meaning that they are

16. Real, "Therapeutic Use of Self," 270.
17. Anderson and Goolishian, "Beyond Cybernetics," 161.
18. Epstein and Loos, "Some Irreverent Thoughts," 415.
19. Kudlac, "Including God in the Conversation," 277–86.
20. Real, "Therapeutic Use of Self," 255–72.

giving to those problems. We are guests in these problem-determined systems. As such, our role rests in the belief that, in order to help these troubled relationships, we must engage the members of these systems in conversations. Within our conversations with these individuals, we must seek to find new meanings and new constructions for the stories of their lives.

2

Toward a Theology of Hope

*Speaking the Goodness of God
in a Pathological Culture*

A RECURRING THEME IN the pastoral counseling literature focuses on the integration of theology and psychology. Volumes of books, articles, and research center on the debate of how these two domains should or should not relate. University and seminary graduate programs offer degrees in the Integration of Psychology and Theology. The *Journal of Psychology and Theology*, published by the Rosemead School of Psychology at Biola University, has been devoted to publishing research on the topic of integration for over four decades. Students regularly want to know if and how, as pastoral counselors, they can use psychology as a resource from sound theological perspectives.

Perspectives on Integration

Obviously, considering the vast amount of literature on integration, there are innumerable perspectives and applications, as well as differing opinions on how and if theology and modern psychology can or cannot relate. It is important to begin with the realization that, while discussions of theological integration often take place in scholarly circles, the implications of those perspectives influence the development of particular approaches to Christian counseling—approaches that have a genuine impact on how we actually deliver care for individuals and families in distress.

These practical applications of theory range across a spectrum of positions. In their book *Psychology and Christianity: Four Views*, Eric L. Johnson and Stanton L. Jones offer a helpful summative perspective of these conversations: "Christians have taken different positions regarding the extent to which they should have anything to do with modern psychology, some embracing it wholeheartedly, others rejecting it just as vigorously, and many others falling somewhere between."[1]

Opposition to Integration

At one extreme is the view that the Bible holds all the answers needed for life's difficulties. This view refuses, therefore, to consider any psychological insight. The ultra-conservative model of Nouthetic Counseling, developed by Jay Adams, typifies this Bible-only view. Renouncing any psychological insight, Adams and his followers completely oppose any aspect of integration between psychology and theology, believing that the Bible is the caregiver's complete and only resource. Adams explains that he specifically chose the term "Nouthetic," from the Greek term for "admonish," to distinguish his model from other counseling approaches that are simply referred to as "Biblical" or "Christian." He defines this approach as using the Bible for "face to face confrontation by one person to another, out of loving concern for him, in order to bring about the changes God desires in his life."[2]

Support for Integration

The opposite extreme emphasizes that psychological and biblical ideals can function well together. As stated by Bruce Narramore, one of the more influential voices in favor of integration, "[T]hese efforts are based on one essential philosophical underpinning—the

---

1. Johnson and Jones, *Psychology and Christianity*, 9.
2. Adams, "What Is Nouthetic Counseling?" http://www.nouthetic.org/what-is-nouthetic-counseling.

belief that all truth is God's truth, wherever it is found. This proposition is frequently referred to as 'the unity of truth.'"[3]

The Futility of Integration

I don't claim to have read every piece of literature regarding the opposition toward integration, the voices in favor, or the countless conversations espousing views between the two extremes. However, I think I've read enough to make this conclusion: integration is a futile task. I have come to believe that no matter how hard one either twists scripture or reinterprets Freud or any of the neo-Freudians who followed, the two domains are ultimately incommensurable. Clinical psychologist David Schnarch makes the point well: "On one hand modern psychiatry and psychology describe men and women as self-centered, while on the other, they encourage them to be more so."[4]

I simply do not believe that we can integrate that self-centered emphasis with the fundamental assertions of Jesus that "the first will be last"[5] and that "it is more blessed to give than to receive,"[6] or his challenge, "If any want to become my followers, let them deny themselves and take up their cross and follow me."[7] Some have tried to suggest that to "love your neighbor as yourself"[8] means that you have to love yourself first. While I'm not opposed to having a healthy self-image, I think that trying to argue for it from that passage trivializes the central point of Christ's command. Theologian Thomas Oden says it well:

> In the adaptation of modern psychology, the fundament of Christian pastoral care in its classical sense has at best been neglected and at worst polemicized. So, pastoral

3. Carter and Narramore, *Integration of Psychology and Theology*, 13.
4. Schnarch, *Constructing the Sexual Crucible*, 6.
5. Matthew 20:16.
6. Acts 20:35.
7. Matthew 16:24.
8. Mark 12:31.

theology has become in many cases little more than a thoughtless mimic of the most current psychological trends. Often these trends . . . have been [rooted] in bad psychology to begin with. It is little wonder that the working pastor continues to look in vain to the field of pastoral theology for some distinction between Christian pastoral care and popular psychological faddism.[9]

None of this means, however, that I believe pastoral counseling cannot borrow from the tools of psychology. In my own training and practice of counseling, I rely extensively on the theories and techniques that I learned in my secular counseling program. The many good professors I encountered in that program deeply shaped my approach to counseling in every way.

A Diversity of Definitions

My conclusion that integration is a futile task is based on an observation of the character of these positions and the arguments put forth in the literature. My sense of each supporting argument is that the debate often becomes paralyzed in over-generalization, arguing from the all-encompassing and generic terms of "theology" and "psychology." In contrast, it is important to note that, as observed by Bruce Wampold, "[T]here are over 250 distinct psychotherapeutic approaches, which are described in one way or another in over 10,000 books."[10] Likewise, in over 2,000 years of Christian history, there is certainly more than one perspective on theology. I believe that an essential yet rarely asked question for those involved in the integration debate is: Which psychology and which theology are either being integrated or rejected?

There is a developing body of literature that recognizes the great diversity of theological and psychological perspectives that the generic debate tends to overlook. Two works that specifically evaluate numerous models of psychology are *Taking the Word to*

---

9. Oden, *Care of Souls in the Classic Tradition*, 5.
10. Wampold, *Great Psychotherapy Debate*, 1.

Heart by Robert C. Roberts[11] and *Modern Psychotherapies* by Stanton L. Jones and Richard E. Butman[12]. In both of these books, the authors recognize that, particularly when it comes to models of counseling, there is more than one approach. Both offer a concise overview of some of the more prominent approaches to counseling, from psychoanalysis to family therapies, holding each under a lens of theology. While these two works are very clear in presenting and critiquing various views of psychology, they are not as clear in explicating the theological assumptions that ground their critiques. In essence, they begin with specific psychologies and examine them from what I would describe as a generic theology.

The Chalcedonian Pattern

Author Deborah van Deusen Hunsinger acknowledges the need for specifying both theological and psychological assumptions when attempting to navigate the complex integration of the two areas, particularly in the counseling session. Of her early counseling training and experience, Hunsinger states, "To be sure, I had various maps in hand, some constructed by depth psychologists and others drawn up by various theologians and spiritual guides, but how did they all fit together?"[13] Hunsinger then develops what she describes as a "theological compass," which is most helpful in examining individual models of psychology from a more specified theological view. Put simply, Hunsinger finds that "we need a way of orienting ourselves theologically."[14] She finds "such a compass in the church's definition of how the divine and human natures of Jesus Christ are to be conceived and related in the teaching of the church."[15]

---

11. Roberts, *Taking the Word to Heart*.

12. Jones and Butman, *Modern Psycotherapies*.

13. Van Deusen Hunsinger, "Interdisciplinary Map for Christian Counselors," 218.

14. Van Deusen Hunsinger, "Interdisciplinary Map for Christian Counselors," 220.

15. Van Deusen Hunsinger, "Interdisciplinary Map for Christian Counselors," 220.

Referring to the church fathers who gathered at the Council of Chalcedon in A.D. 451, Hunsinger applies a Chalcedonian pattern as a more intentional method for conceiving the relationship between theology and psychology. The central Chalcedonian question centered around how the divine and human natures of Jesus can co-exist without "separation or division on the one hand and without confusion or change on the other."[16] The author asserts that the relational terms of this question are fundamental to her conceptualization of the relationship between theology and psychology. She stresses that the pattern represented in this question about the nature of Christ can be applied to a "wide range of other questions,"[17] serving as a "grammar"[18] or a template for understanding the relational aspects of distinct areas.

Hunsinger explains that there are three formal features of the Chalcedonian pattern that can enlighten our perception of the divinity and humanity of Jesus. 1) *Indissoluble differentiation* refers to the reality that Jesus is both fully divine and fully human. These two natures of Jesus are in a relationship in which they exist together, but one nature cannot be confused or changed by the other, so that they remain "indissolubly differentiated."[19] 2) *Inseparable unity* notes that while the two natures are ultimately different, they are also mysteriously united in the miracle of the incarnation—Jesus is fully human; Jesus is fully divine. While he is of two natures, the two natures are perfectly united in one Christ. 3) *Indestructible order* refers to a "logical priority or precedence"[20] of Christ's divine nature over his human nature. Hunsinger stresses that this logical priority does not

---

16. Van Deusen Hunsinger, "Interdisciplinary Map for Christian Counselors," 221.

17. Van Deusen Hunsinger, "Interdisciplinary Map for Christian Counselors," 221.

18. Van Deusen Hunsinger, "Interdisciplinary Map for Christian Counselors," 221.

19. Van Deusen Hunsinger, "Interdisciplinary Map for Christian Counselors," 222.

20. Van Deusen Hunsinger, "Interdisciplinary Map for Christian Counselors," 224.

"subordinate"[21] Christ's humanity to his divinity. Rather, in understanding the unity of the two natures, the Chalcedonian conception also attends to the notion of a "pre-existent divine Logos, who was with God before the foundation of the world,"[22] and thus, the divine nature of Christ logically precedes his humanity.

While an exposition of the Chalcedonian pattern offers a richly edifying perspective for thinking about the doctrine of Christ, for Hunsinger and for the purposes of this discussion, it is also informative to the debate of psychological/theological integration. Hunsinger deftly applies the template to this concern.

Indissoluble Differentiation

Hunsinger observes that psychology and theology are 1) *indissolubly differentiated*, and that it is a mistake to consider them somehow "interchangeable."[23] Although the two fields may speak to the same issues of human struggle, they do so from different fields of inquiry, operate from independent assumptions and theories, and have distinct vocabularies. For example, Hunsinger argues that it would be a serious mistake to equate a client's psychological symptoms with sin, as if we were simply using different terminology to speak of the same problem:

> Psychology and theology are logically diverse, they have different aims, subject matters, methods and linguistic conventions. It is one thing, for instance, to think of oneself as beset with a terrible "negative mother complex" and as needing to learn to trust one's feminine side; it is quite another to think of oneself as mistrusting God's providential goodness and needing to confess the sin of

---

21. Van Deusen Hunsinger, "Interdisciplinary Map for Christian Counselors," 225.

22. Van Deusen Hunsinger, "Interdisciplinary Map for Christian Counselors," 225.

23. Van Deusen Hunsinger, "Interdisciplinary Map for Christian Counselors," 222.

unbelief. Yet both ways of conceiving oneself and one's predicament might be apt in a particular case.[24]

Inseparable Unity

Hunsinger next states that the two fields of psychology and theology are also 2) *inseparably united*—not, of course, inseparable in this instance as in the incarnation of Christ, but inseparable by the simple fact that our lives are not compartmentalized into spiritual and psychological categories. It is an important realization for a Christian counselor to understand that the problems people bring to us are both temporal and spiritual. If I am struggling in the relationship I have with my spouse, that struggle is also spiritual, impacting and being impacted by my relationship with God. Developments in the field of counseling are calling greater attention—even in the secular literature—to the importance of including clients' spirituality as a helping resource.[25] That some discussions in the integration literature indiscriminately differentiate the human problem into these two categories is, I think, detrimental to the care of the soul.

Indestructible Order

Finally, Hunsinger applies the notion of 3) *indestructible order* to the integration of theology and psychology. This third element of the Chalcedonian pattern offers important balance to how the Christian counselor incorporates the resources of psychology into the care of others: it gives preeminence to the rule of God in all our lives. As an educator in the field of pastoral care and counseling, I often stress to students that in forming their personal approach to counseling, they need to learn to discriminate "good psychology" from "bad psychology." Making these distinctions requires a pastoral heart that begins with a theological question: Who is God?

---

24. Van Deusen Hunsinger, *Theology and Pastoral Counseling*, 5.
25. See Kudlac, "Including God in the Conversation."

Practical Application of the Chalcedonian Pattern

As a demonstration in applying the Chalcedonian pattern to a particular context, Hunsinger discusses the miraculous healing of the paralytic in Mark 2:8–12:

> At once Jesus perceived in his spirit that they were discussing these questions among themselves; and he said to them, "Why do you raise such questions in your hearts? Which is easier, to say to the paralytic, 'Your sins are forgiven,' or to say, 'Stand up and take your mat and walk'? But so that you may know that the Son of Man has authority on earth to forgive sins"—he said to the paralytic— "I say to you, stand up, take your mat and go to your home." And he stood up, and immediately took the mat and went out before all of them; so that they were all amazed and glorified God, saying, "We have never seen anything like this!"[26]

Explaining that the three elements of the Chalcedonian pattern can be observed in this account of a theological act (the forgiveness of sin) and a physical act (the healing of paralysis), Hunsinger observes that 1) the forgiveness of the paralytic's sin and his healing are *inseparable* in the miraculous cure from Christ; 2) they are, however, *differentiated* (one has to do with the man's spiritual condition, the other with the physical capacity to walk); and 3) there is *divine order* in that Jesus, with the authority to forgive the man's sin, also has the authority to heal his paralysis.

The value of the Chalcedonian pattern as a template for thinking about the relationship between psychology and theology is that it suggests a space for the Christian counselor to use the resources of psychology that are consistent with theological wisdom, with the insights of the Christian traditions of pastoral care, and with a preeminence for biblical teaching. Within the conceptualization of 1) *indissoluble differentiation*, the Chalcedonian pattern allows for a distinction between psychology and theology. One does not have to choose one or the other. The concept of 2)

---

26. Mark 2:8–12.

inseparable unity within the pattern recognizes that, in caring for others, the two fields have much in common and can be used in complementary fashion. And the idea of 3) *divine order* can help to keep us accountable to the logical and proper hierarchy of theology over psychology.

I want to stress that this presentation of the Chalcedonian pattern as a rubric for understanding a relationship between theology and psychology is not, I hope, a mere rationalization to defend my preferred model of counseling. On the contrary, I am disturbed by the lengths to which some writers go in trying to "baptize" a secular model for Christian use. The template of the Chalcedonian pattern as presented by Hunsinger gives greater honor to scripture by allowing the use of an idea from a secular realm without having to twist a passage out of context to argue biblical precedence. Frankly, I don't think that Solution-Focused Counseling, the model I'm advocating in this book, is located in the Bible. While I believe and hope that the pastoral caregiver's life will be rooted in God and informed by scripture, I think it trivializes the text if we force it to illustrate a principle of which the biblical writer probably had no awareness.

In Defense of Solution-Focused Counseling

So, rather than attempt to support the value of Solution-Focused Counseling in a way that might devalue the biblical text, I propose that the suitability of the approach is evidenced in the opportunities it provides for the pastoral counselor to be helpful to parishioners. The Solution-Focused model offers those who are hurting a language of hope in ways that traditional psychology and pastoral care have not made available.

These opportunities for helpful conversations in a ministry of pastoral care are at the heart of Solution-Focused Counseling.[27]

---

27. A number of authors in the field of pastoral care are discovering the value of this model. See the bibliography for a list of books and articles that, in my view, are some of the best presentations.

A story from my own counseling experience may help to illustrate these perspectives.[28]

A ten-year-old boy was having ongoing difficulty managing himself at school and was in trouble daily for disrupting his class. Over time, the frustration mounted with the teacher suspecting that the boy had Attention Deficit Hyperactivity Disorder (ADHD). The teacher called in the school principal, who agreed with the teacher and decided to bring in the mother for consultation. As the meeting proceeded, the mother resented the accusations about her son, resisted the diagnosis of ADHD, and (from the view of school personnel) was uncooperative. The meeting escalated, so the principal finally gave an ultimatum: "Either you will get your son on some sort of medication or find some way for him to behave, or he will not be allowed to stay in the classroom." As a last-ditch compromise, the school system agreed to let her try counseling—as long as there was significant improvement.

To define his problem as merely a psychological or even organic disorder would, in my mind, have been to settle for an explanation that focused only on the little boy as a problem from a linear diagnosis. Instead, I began with a belief that the school, the family, and even the little boy were participants in a view that characterized him as a "trouble-maker."

I opened our first counseling session with a Solution-Focused perspective, asking him if there were ever any times when he didn't get in trouble. This counseling technique is referred to as "exception-building."[29] He responded by describing a day earlier that school year when he was sick and stayed home from school. He and his mother spent that day playing games and reading together on his bed. In his explanation, he stated that he did not get in trouble all day long. I responded, "So, maybe you aren't a bad kid. Maybe you are just a lonely kid." His mother reacted beautifully by structuring a plan to spend just a few more minutes with him each day.

---

28. Details of this account have been altered and combined with other cases to protect confidentiality.

29. "Exception-building" is explained further in chapter 4.

Over the course of the next few weeks, our counseling sessions concentrated on finding other instances when, although the opportunities for him to misbehave were available, he managed to avoid getting in trouble. At one point I asked if there were any times when he knew that he was going to get in trouble before it happened.[30] He informed me that there were times when he could "see trouble coming."

Another approach that is often useful in Solution-Focused Counseling is known as "externalizing" the problem.[31] Grounded in a postmodern counseling approach, this technique from Narrative Therapy assumes that the counselee *has a relationship with* the problem, rather than assuming that he *is* the problem. In actuality, everyone involved in this situation—the parents, the school personnel, and even I, as the counselor—had a relationship with the problem. It was that relationship that needed to change.

In this instance, I believed that the "problem" was controlling the little boy (and everyone else involved), so we needed to structure a change in the relationship that would put him in control. I proposed that on Thursday at 2:00 p.m., he invite what we began to refer to as the "trouble monster" to come in and cause him to misbehave. I assured him that there would be no consequences from the teacher; I would ask for her permission for him to allow a visit from the trouble monster. The joy at being given permission to misbehave brought a devilish grin to his face. But in a wonderfully ironic turn, when I asked him at the next session how it went letting the trouble monster pay a visit, his response was simply, "I decided that I didn't want to let him in this time." With the suggestion that he could be more in control of his behavior than the trouble monster, his behavior at school continued to change. A revised story of this little boy emerged that characterized him as a cooperative and positive element in his class.

I don't present this case to suggest that all treatments for ADHD or any other psychologically defined problems are simple. Moreover, I don't intend to minimize the seriousness of deep

---

30. This is more "exception-building."
31. See White and Epston, *Narrative Means to Therapeutic Ends*, 38.

psychological issues. What I will propose is that, in reframing the definition of the boy from "trouble-maker" to "lonely," and in focusing on instances when he behaved rather than only misbehaved, we were able to introduce a change into the negative perception of the boy as a behavior problem.

We can also consider this case in light of the Chalcedonian template as proposed by Hunsinger. Doing so will help to demonstrate the theological/psychological beneficence of the Solution-Focused model. Like the paralytic in the gospel of Mark, this young boy was trapped in a condition that characterized his existence, how people perceived him, and how others related to him. The conceptualization of 1) *indissoluble differentiation* in the Chalcedonian pattern permitted me, as the counselor to this young man, to use resources and techniques that come from the field of psychology. But the concept of 2) *inseparable unity* within the pattern allowed me to recognize that this young man's dilemma was not just a problem for psychology. Actually, I believe that psychology was *contributing* to his problem; in this instance, what I view as "bad psychology" was labeling him with a diagnosis of ADHD, which ignored other possibilities for his behavior. I believe that "good psychology" will be consistent with good theology. From a theological perspective, this young man, like the paralytic, was released from the oppression of his problem. The Solution-Focused approach made other definitions of his problem besides the traditional psychological diagnosis possible, and it allowed a change in his relationship to the trouble monster. As this relationship changed, the dominance of the problem-focused system changed its story.

I don't make the claim that the Solution-Focused approach is the only theologically consistent model of counseling, nor is it necessarily always compatible with theology.[32] The Chalcedonian idea of 3) *divine order* is most useful as a reminder of the logical and proper hierarchy of theology over psychology in examining for this compatibility. I will argue that one aspect of that hierarchy

---

32. See chapter 4 on the assumptions of Solution-Focused Counseling for this discussion.

must be a preeminent place for the gospel to work in the life of the counselee. Good psychology will always be consistent with the possibility for God's redeeming work in this world. Good counseling grounded in good theology will work to find ways to open the door for God's liberating presence.

In the conclusion of his book *Solution-Focused Pastoral Counseling*, author Charles Kollar summarizes this perspective well: "Being labeled by an expert on mental disorders and hearing him use deficiency language often locks the counselee into his problems and disorientation. But as counselors we must remind ourselves that the counselee is a child of God with his own dreams and hopes."[33] Solution-Focused approaches to pastoral conversation are at their very best when they speak this hope and bring the counselee into the goodness of this God.

---

33. Kollar, *Solution-Focused Pastoral Counseling*, 215.

3

The Magic of Language

*Hope-Filled Conversations
in Pastoral Care*

HEINZ VON FOERSTER, a biologist and frequent contributor to the field of family therapy, described an opportunity he was given to visit a counseling session:

> I was invited to sit in the observation room and to watch through a one-way mirror a therapeutic session in progress with a family of four. At one moment my colleagues had to leave, and I was by myself. I was curious as to what I would see when I could not hear what was said, so I turned the sound off. What I saw then, the silent pantomime, the parting and closing of lips, the body movements, the boy who only once stopped biting his nails . . . What I saw were the dance steps of language, the dance steps alone, without the disturbing effects of the music. What magic, I thought, must sit in the noises these people produced by pushing air past their vocal cords, and by parting and closing their lips.[1]

The magic of language, and particularly its influence in shaping our lives, is the essence of this book. It is our great privilege, as counselors, to be invited into the private lives and languages of the individuals and families in our care. Along with that privilege, we have the enormous responsibility of joining the conversation of our counselees with humility and respect for the places they

---

1. Von Foerster, "Ethics and Second-Order Cybernetics."

open to us. I firmly believe that the Christian counselor has the resources of a language that can introduce hope and possibility into the lives of broken people; the approach to counseling presented in this work rests on that belief. Where contemporary psychology often diagnoses and pathologizes the human dilemma, the good news of the Christian gospel is that Christ sets those who are imprisoned by oppressive words free into the love and mercy of a caring God.

The Difficulty of Talking about Language

There is, however, an inherently difficult and paradoxical challenge to the endeavor of this discussion: the attempt to explain language cannot be made without words. To explain how words function and impact our experience of the world, the only means we have available is language. Words are the tools for describing how we use words. In his essay "Ethics and Second-Order Cybernetics," von Foerster recounts a story from anthropologist Margaret Mead of an experience that illustrates the ultimate absurdity of using language to explain language. In working to understand the colloquial languages of the tribes she studied, she would often point to objects and wait for the appropriate sound that was the corresponding word for the item in that particular language. In one instance of using this pointing technique, she kept getting the same response for every item she pointed to: "chu mulu." Her initial conclusion was that this was a very primitive language with a tiny vocabulary. Later she learned that in the language she was researching, "chu mulu" means "pointing with finger."[2]

Another way to explain this is to say that words are symbols. For example, the word "table" refers to a flat surface that is attached to some sort of structure beneath that raises it off the floor and keeps it steady. Actually, the word "table" is a combination of letters that produce a sound that a speaker uses as a shortcut to keep from having to repeatedly string a longer list of symbols together to try

---

2. Von Foerster, "Ethics and Second-Order Cybernetics."

to communicate what is meant by "table." The combination of the letters T-A-B-L-E is, in essence, our socially agreed-on symbol and shortcut for that particular structure. In Spanish, the combination of the letters M-E-S-A symbolizes the same object that the English language symbolizes with the letters T-A-B-L-E, so the meaning of the word is the symbol accepted by those who speak the particular language. The point in all of this is to recognize that words gain their meaning through their use in social interchange within the language practice of the culture.

The Language of Contemporary Psychology

In his 1991 work *The Saturated Self*, author Kenneth Gergen[3] encourages readers to think of some of the terms for understanding the human being that have found their way into daily conversation in our lifetimes. Distinctions that would have been foreign half a century ago are now a part of everyday jargon. Words like self-esteem, significant other, inner-child, dysfunctional family, panic disorder, repressed memory, anorexia, bulimia, and an assortment of others have become household terms. In actuality, like "table," these words have become our agreed-on symbols for depicting those human functions.

Put simply, the ideas of modern psychology have gradually been absorbed into the life of the larger society. In describing this phenomenon, Mary Pipher observes,

> Psychology is everywhere. Small-town people talk about low self-esteem, depression, panic disorders, and Freudian slips. Truck drivers go to therapists and waitresses analyze one another's dreams . . . by the 1990's popular psychology was on radio and T.V. talk shows, in women's magazines and presidential speeches . . . We baby boomers seem obsessed with taking our emotional temperature at every turn."[4]

3. Gergen, *Saturated Self*, 13.
4. Pipher, *Shelter of Each Other*, 93.

I believe that in our modern quest for human potential and individual fulfillment, the language of contemporary psychology has created unrealistic expectations for personal happiness. For the sake of contrast, I think of my father. He was born in 1923 and grew up in a time before these ways of speaking about ourselves were absorbed into our self-understanding. He was the third of seven children; two of his brothers died in early childhood. He had vivid memories of the Depression, of World War II, of life before television, and of a house without indoor plumbing. He liked to tell his grandchildren about life on his grandfather's farm, where the children rode on the backs of pigs that would try to brush them off by running under the house.

From my father's perspective, "Life was not better or worse back then. It was just different." His generation handled pain, heartache, and personal difficulty in a more discreet way. Problems weren't something they necessarily talked about, and they certainly wouldn't pay someone a hundred dollars an hour to listen to their problems. They kept their problems to themselves. They prayed, or they talked to relatives. I don't believe that keeping our emotions to ourselves or telling people to "just deal with it" is the best way to handle problems. What I do question is the enshrinement of psychology as the solution to all our problems. As quoted in chapter 2, author David Schnarch makes the important observation that "[o]n the one hand modern psychiatry and psychology describe men and women as self-centered, while on the other, they encourage them to be more so."[5]

In these psychological ways of speaking about our lives, there is often an unquestioned acceptance of a medical model of health care as the definitive way to also understand mental health. This medical perspective on mental health is most clearly depicted in the *Diagnostic and Statistical Manual of Mental Disorders* (DSM), published by the American Psychiatric Association.[6] The DSM-5 is widely used by mental health professionals, insurance companies,

---

5. Schnarch, *Constructing the Sexual Crucible*, 6.

6. American Psychiatric Association, *Diagnostic and Statistical Manual of Mental Disorders*.

and the judicial system. In essence, it serves as the catalog of diagnostic criteria for possible diagnoses that a psychologist can make. These diagnoses are often given through a process of elimination in which the professional considers how many symptoms a person exhibits for a particular diagnosis. In the most recent edition of the manual, there are a total of 297 possible diagnoses that range from disorders such as "Schizophrenia" or "Major Depression" to more obscure designations such as "Hypoactive Sexual Desire." For the sake of contrast, the 1917 classification system identified only fifty-nine forms of mental disorder.[7] In short, we've become obsessed with psychological diagnoses, and our vocabulary reflects this.

The Language of Psychology in the Church

That this dynamic of our culture has also infiltrated our churches is particularly disturbing. One of the fathers of pastoral care, Charles Gerkin, comments,

> Pastors who became acquainted with psychological and psychotherapeutic ways of thinking about human problems . . . have taught their people psychological ways of speaking about everything from the childhood origins of adult human difficulty to the stages in the processes of death and bereavement . . . At their best, these pastoral activities have been able to bring the values and meanings of the Christian tradition into dialogue with contemporary culture. At their worst, these activities have tended to subordinate the gospel to the latest package of popular psychology.[8]

The question that these developments raise for those who offer pastoral care is whether this emphasis on diagnosing mental disorders is encouraging people in our society toward greater mental health or leading people to greater self-preoccupation. It

---

7. Adamowicz, "Diagnostic and Statistical Manual of Mental Disorders," https://www.mentalhelp.net/articles/diagnostic-and-statistical-manual-of-mental-disorders/.

8. Gerkin, *Introduction to Pastoral Care*, 95.

can perhaps be argued that our sensitivity to the psychological maladies of the human condition is becoming more astute, that life is increasingly complicated, and that naming the ills that confound us is the first step in treating them. On the other hand, we might need to ask if our society is simply absorbed in a perpetual "navel gaze." I don't know if we are becoming more sensitive or just more self-absorbed, but I'm far more interested in a different question: How, in a culture that is indoctrinated in psychology and self-help literature, can we have good conversations that point people toward realistic ways of dealing with the challenges of life?

It seems that our society, and oftentimes our churches, are enamored by the claim that life's most difficult problems call for psychological treatment. I believe that God is at work in the psychological sciences, and an insight or strategy from this resource can be a powerful tool in the hands of people of faith who wish to bring healing, wholeness, and reconciliation. If, however, in offering pastoral care in our churches, the primary focus is upon psychological diagnosis and its approaches to treatment, we may entirely miss the call and demand of God—the God who gives direction and power to change people, to make us whole, and to experience the liberation of living in God's Kingdom. As pastoral counselors, we have the responsibility of caring for individuals who are caught in the maladies and struggles of modern life. The rather lofty goal of this book is to offer counselors a different model of psychological treatment than the dominant and often pathologizing perspectives represented by the DSM.

New Ways of Speaking

The thesis of this work is based on the essential observation that language constructs psychology and, therefore, that we must be very intentional about how we construct, or how we "talk," in pastoral care. I don't claim that these approaches to pastoral care are the only correct method, or that they are timeless. In fact, they are in flux as I write because they are contained in language and expressed in language. And within this limitation of language lies an exciting opportunity: the possibility of finding new, life-giving ways of speaking in pastoral counseling that are not bound by the pathological constraints of medical diagnosis. As author Glen Boyd observes, "Our ultimate relatedness to God takes place in the context of radical non-pathologizing grace in which God accepts us without judgment, even with a DSM diagnosis. Rather, God-in-Christ participates with us in a hope-filled conversation toward salvation and wholeness."[9]

Up to this point, I have attempted to provide both a theoretical and theological framework for conducting pastoral care from a position that offers those who are struggling renewed hope for change in their lives. Rather than an emphasis on diagnostic expertise that depends on expert knowledge of pathological symptoms, the model of counseling that I present in the coming chapters emphasizes that others know more about their lives than I do. The challenge for the counselor who comes alongside those in his or her care is to seek to truly hear and understand their realities.

With that emphasis, I turn now to an approach to counseling that values good listening and genuine respect for the other. Rather than defining and diagnosing problems, this approach constructs hopeful discussion focused on discovering positive solutions.

---

9. Boyd, "Kerygma and Conversation," 161.

4

The Basics of Solution-Focused Counseling

As mentioned in the preface of this work, I've been honored over the years to bring this material to a variety of churches and lay pastoral care trainees, to college and high school peer counselor groups, to congregational leaders, to ministry teams, and to seminary students. What follows in this chapter is drawn from those presentations in a way that I hope will offer the reader a practical guide for developing materials that will be helpful in training others to use the Solution-Focused Model of Counseling.

I have found that a particularly important aspect of this training is teaching the Solution-Focused Model of Counseling from a Solution-Focused frame of reference. More will be said about the various assumptions and techniques of the model, but I also want to stress that these same techniques are helpful in teaching the model to others. For example, in debriefing role plays and other exercises, I consistently frame the conversation toward encouraging trainees to notice what they do well, I focus on strengths that they demonstrate, and when they identify weaknesses in their counseling skills, we work to help them find exceptions to those limitations—all of which are techniques of the method. This approach encourages trainees to think about ways they are gifted for this ministry, to find their own styles and rhythms for connecting with people, and to discover next steps that will help them continue to develop as helpful caregivers.

With this perspective in mind, I offer an overview of the basic assumptions of Solution- Focused Theory, along with examples of how I have attempted to help groups of trainees grasp these ideas. I end this chapter with an overview of Solution-Focused techniques, discussing how counselors might use them in the process of a counseling session.

Assumptions of Solution-Focused Counseling

The origins of Solution-Focused counseling can be traced back to the practice of Steve de Shazer, Insoo Kim Berg, and colleagues at the Brief Family Therapy Center in Milwaukee, Wisconsin. Their long-held belief that "holistically observing and reflecting on the actual process in which they work with their clients will teach them more about how to be effective than will traditional scientific research"[1] generated this alternate approach, which has now been developing since the mid-1980s. The following core assumptions are foundational to understanding the Solution-Focused model.

Assumption #1: The Counselee Is the "Expert"

A fundamental frame of reference with which I begin each counseling relationship is that if the family or individual has reached the point where they are frustrated enough with their problem that they would consult someone who is identified as a helpful resource they have, in a certain sense, run out of other ideas. I also begin with the awareness that people in the midst of perplexing problems often develop a tunnel vision view of the issue. Unsure what else to do, they simply try harder with the solutions that have already not worked. I presented a counseling conversation in chapter 2 in which a little boy was being labeled with ADHD. In this situation, the frustrations with the boy led the teacher, who found that she

---

1. De Jong and Berg, *Interviewing for Solutions*, 11.

could not control him, to seek the higher authority of the principal to do what she could not. When the principal experienced the same exasperation, she turned to the parents as the greater authority, demanding that they enforce what the school had been unable to accomplish. As a last resort, the parents were allowed to find another authority to turn to. I became the next authority in this chain of people who would have a chance to manage the boy. As such, I began with the realization that the position of authority in this instance had basically been subverted by the (like it or not) more powerful uncontrollable behavior of the boy.

Rather than more exasperation and defeat, the Solution-Focused perspective accepts this alternate chain of command with the assumption that the client is the expert on her problem. While we as counselors may have training and expertise in dealing with human problems, we do not know more about what it is like to be that person or to bear that problem. This little boy knew more about his relationship with the trouble monster than any amount of training could ever have provided me. Recognizing his expert status on the problem also communicated to him that he was competent to manage his behavior. I think that was an important message for him because, up until that point, the messages had only communicated that he was apparently not able to manage himself.

In public presentations of these concepts, I find that a question frequently arises from participants: "Does speaking of the problem this way excuse the individual—such as this young man—from personal responsibility for his bad behavior? Does naming the 'trouble monster' as something he has a relationship with absolve him of the consequences for his uncooperative presence in the classroom?" This line of questioning seems to come from a concern that the individual needs to somehow be aware of his responsibility and even convinced that he is guilty in his behavior. My experience has been that individuals are painfully aware of the distress their actions bring to others and that they often feel helpless, hopeless, and distraught by those consequences.

The dominant story about this young man was that he was a problem. His teacher, his principal, and his classmates were unanimous in their blame. He had been accused, punished, and taunted. He had been labeled difficult, out-of-control, and a problem student. I do not think he needed to be convinced to feel bad. In contrast, I believe that talking to him in a way that suggested he was the expert on his behavior helped him to be responsible, even more so than the tactic of trying to manage him had done, and particularly more than the suggested solution of medicating his behavior could have. Through the suggestion that he had a relationship with his bad behavior and that he was the expert on that relationship, he was empowered to be responsible where previous attempts to control his behavior had failed. Michael White and David Epston suggest a similar dynamic in their conversation regarding clients who have been required to attend counseling: "Helping people separate from the problem and assessing it objectively can help them assume responsibility for it."[2]

The assumption that the counselee is the expert on his problem is a common perspective in other postmodern discussions of counseling. For example, Anderson and Goolishian highlight this understanding in the article "The Client is the Expert: A Not Knowing Approach to Therapy."[3] These authors stress that "Not Knowing" refers to how the counselor functions to make it possible for meanings and stories to unfold in collaboration with the counselee. Freedman and Combs add that this perspective "implies not asking questions from a position of pre-understanding and not asking questions to which we want particular answers." Instead, they assert that we should assume "an 'I don't know anything' position," adding that "[o]ur knowledge is of the process of therapy, not the content and meaning of people's lives."[4]

---

2. White and Epston, *Narrative Means to Therapeutic Ends*, 65.
3. Anderson and Goolishian, "Client is the Expert," 25–39.
4. Freedman and Combs, *Narrative Therapy*, 44.

Assumption #2: A Positive, Future-Focused Outlook Leads to Change

Focusing on the positive, on the future, and on the solution facilitates change in the desired direction. In the instance of the little boy, attention had been given *ad infinitum* to his negative behavior; one could certainly make the argument that he was not suffering from a deficit of attention. Rather, the excess of attention he was receiving was all concentrated on his negative acting out. The alternative method of focusing on instances when he did not get in trouble, or when he was able to see trouble coming, allowed a future-directed vision of what life would be like when the problem was not a problem anymore. This future-directed emphasis centered on conversations about what he would be doing when the problem was no longer present.

These types of conversations often result in being able to form mental representations of the solution. I asked the little boy to think about what he would see himself doing if he were cooperating in the classroom. One of the ways the trouble monster had been allowed to persist was that *not* misbehaving as a goal was only oriented toward *stopping* bad behavior. The future-directed line of questioning, on the other hand, allowed him to imagine what he might be doing instead of getting in trouble.

Assumption #3: There Is an Exception to Every Problem

Within our conversations, we can find and create exceptions to every problem. This assumption—believing that even the worst problem does not occur all the time—is fundamental to building hope for the counselee. The little boy was getting in trouble a lot, and his classroom disruptions were obviously controlling much of the teacher's time. But there were at least brief times when he was not disruptive. Even the occasion when he stayed home with his mother all day allowed room for the alternate view that there were times when he did not get in trouble. Detailing these exceptions as times when he was behaving opened the possibility for him to reframe his conduct and question the pervasive view that he was *totally* out-of-control.

It is interesting to note that even the DSM-5 list of symptoms that constitute Attention Deficit/Hyperactivity Disorder allows the opportunity to notice exceptions. The DSM states:

> Six or more of the following symptoms of inattention have been present for at least 6 months to a point that is disruptive and inappropriate for the developmental level:
>
> - Often fails to give close attention to details or makes careless mistakes in schoolwork, at work, or with other activities.
> - Often has trouble holding attention on tasks or play activities.
> - Often does not seem to listen when spoken to directly.
> - Often does not follow through on instructions and fails to finish schoolwork, chores, or duties in the workplace (e.g., loses focus, side-tracked).
> - Often has trouble organizing tasks and activities.
> - Often avoids, dislikes, or is reluctant to do tasks that require mental effort over a long period of time (such as schoolwork or homework).
> - Often loses things necessary for tasks and activities (e.g., school materials, pencils, books, tools, wallets, keys, paperwork, eyeglasses, mobile telephones).
> - Is often easily distracted.
> - Is often forgetful in daily activities.[5]

Notice that each of these nine descriptions of inattentive behavior includes the word "often." In other words, it was possible that

---

5. National Center on Birth Defects and Developmental Disabilities, "Attention Deficit/Hyperactivity Disorder (ADHD)," https://www.cdc.gov/ncbddd/adhd/diagnosis.html.

although this young man was "often" inattentive, there might be exceptions to his inattention. The very diagnosis being used to define him leaves room to notice occasions when he was attentive or, at least, less disruptive. "Often" intrinsically suggests the reality that no problem occurs all the time. Additionally, the DSM states that six or more of the nine symptoms must be present. Rather than an absolute diagnosis or definitive reality that the little boy either had or did not have ADHD, even the American Psychiatric Association leaves room for the possibility that problems are rarely characterized as either/or. Problems instead occur on a continuum, leaving room between "always" and "never" for even the smallest exceptions, or times when the problem is not as bad or even not present at all. Was it possible that although the young man was "often easily distracted," he occasionally paid some attention in daily activities?

Further opportunities for noticing exceptions within these descriptions can be found in the subjective nature of the symptom. For example, how does one measure "close attention?" The student sitting two desks over may be sound asleep, but since he is not being disruptive, he will not be suspect in his lack of attention. The diagnostic descriptions of the DSM are generalized, all-encompassing frames of reference that, when broken down into specific instances of behavior, allow for alternate diagnoses that are rarely absolute.

Assumption #4: Change Is Occurring All the Time

In the midst of an overwhelming problem, it is difficult to imagine that life can ever change or be different. Solution-Focused conversations grounded in a process model of living assume, on the other hand, that change is occurring all the time. This idea is consistent with the earlier illustration of feedback in the cybernetic system of the heating and cooling system (see chapter 1). Rather than staying at a fixed temperature, the system maintains itself as the thermostat regulates around the selected temperature. Similarly, the statement "the little boy was in trouble a lot" describes a pattern of behavior. It does *not* describe a static, unchanging condition.

Assumption #5: Small Change Leads to Bigger Change

Because this approach to counseling assumes that change is occurring all the time, one of the goals of the counselor is to facilitate even the smallest change in the right direction. One of the measures that Solution-Focused Counseling encourages is to focus on the member of the problem-defined system who seems most motivated or most likely to cooperate. Encouraging even a small change in this motivated member often begins to reframe the problem for the entire system. In this instance, the parents and the little boy were clearly motivated, whereas the authorities at the school, in their exasperation with the little boy, had abdicated all responsibility and basically communicated that either his behavior had to change or he would be removed from the class. When the teacher noticed the boy being a little more in control of himself, her view of him began to change. This instigated a new pattern in the system in which she affirmed his good behavior, which reinforced his self-management, which led to more good behavior, and so on.

Assumption #6: Clients Are Not Uncooperative

When we encounter resistance, this simply means we have not yet understood the client's view of how change takes place. A fundamental issue of almost all counseling theories is the question of how to deal with client resistance. E. Thomas Dowd notes, "Occasionally, despite a counselor's best efforts, some clients fail to act in their best interests and negatively respond to all counseling interventions. These clients are often called oppositional, reactionary, noncompliant, intractable, and unmotivated."[6] Benjamin Pope defines resistance as "a process of avoiding or diminishing the self-disclosing

---

6. Dowd, "Stasis and Change in Cognitive Psychotherapy," 139–58.

communication requested by the interviewer because of its capacity to make the interviewee uncomfortable or anxious."[7]

In contrast, and consistent with its assumption that the client is the expert on her problem, Solution-Focused Counseling believes that resistance is not a client issue. Rather, it is a problem of the counselor who has in some way failed to understand the view of the individual he is seeking to help. This assumption is grounded in a view that seeks to honor the counselee, recognizing that people who invite us into their private worlds would not do so if they did not actually want us to help.

Assumption #7: People Have the Resources to Solve Their Problems

Solution-Focused Theory, in its emphasis on honoring and believing in the counselee, assumes that somewhere within the counselee's history of dealing with problems, or within her social network, or somewhere within her grasp are the resources for managing her difficulties. It is important to stress that this view does *not* mean that solutions are simple. Nor is this assumption a power-of-positive-thinking trivialization of life's difficulties. Some have critiqued the assumption as a humanistic value, and it certainly has the possibility of being applied as an affirmation of self-reliance and human possibility. However, I think that, particularly within a frame of reference of Christian faith, this assumption affirms the hope that even in life's darkest moments, there is a God who cares and will come alongside those who are broken in this world. In a faith-based application, this assumption can encourage individuals beset with problems to not just rely on their own strength, but to turn to others for help and to seek God's sustaining presence in their lives.

There are many important implications of these assumptions. Among these is the implication that they offer a constructive way

---

7. Pope, *Mental Health Interview*, 74.

of talking with counselees, without relying on the diagnostic tools of the more traditional mental health approaches. As such, the Solution-Focused Model is accessible to those who are willing to approach conversations in ways that honor the perceived reality of those in their care.

The Importance of Listening Well

My strong belief is that, above all else, good listening should characterize these conversations. While listening well is not unique to the Solution-Focused approach, it is certainly integral to this model in its emphasis on the counselee as the expert on his problem. For us to be helpful caregivers, we need to hear and understand the counselee's experiences and beliefs about the problem. We work to see it through his eyes.

In training, I begin with instruction and practice in skills of good listening. I often ask participants how they know they are being listened to in conversations. They tell me that good listeners maintain eye contact, lean forward, do not interrupt, ask clarifying questions, and so on. These responses provide the necessary steps to good listening.

I also emphasize that listening well rests in our capacity to manage ourselves in some of these basic elements of helping conversations:

Managing Our Need to Be Helpful

Understanding our personal motives for engaging in this care and managing any self-centered needs is important in protecting the counseling relationship. It is personally affirming to be appreciated for the help we give, but seeking that affirmation out of some insecurity or unmet need in ourselves impedes our ability to give good care.

Controlling Our Personal Anxiety when People Become Angry

Certainly, we can work to help counselees express anger in helpful ways. But if the anger of others can trigger our own personal issues, we will not be able to understand their views of the world.

Curbing Our Discomfort when Others Cry

It is not unusual for a trainee to want to comfort those who are in distress, putting an arm on their shoulder or offering a Kleenex. Irrespective of motives, these expressions of comfort often communicate our own anxiety and discomfort with tears and can suggest that people should not be upset. Allowing people to express their emotions and to comfort themselves demonstrates our support for them and helps them process what they are experiencing in healthy ways.

Being Comfortable with Silence

When it is time for me to present this skill to trainees, I simply stop talking and wait for the room to become uncomfortable enough that someone "breaks the silence." Then we discuss the discomfort people sometimes feel in moments of silence and the fact that allowing for it in counseling conversations gives people time to process what they are thinking and to formulate their thoughts. Allowing silence also communicates to counselees that they have responsibility and influence in the conversation.

The Discipline of Pausing Our Internal Dialogue

As we listen in normal conversation, we are, at the same time, also thinking about what we will say in response. I believe that listening for understanding requires that we give all of our attention to what the other person is saying. It is a learned discipline to stop the mental process of constructing what we will say next while the other is talking. One effect this practice has is that, as we give all of our attention to what others are saying, they sense our concentration and desire to truly understand them. After they have completed their statement, we construct what we will say. I have seen that this practice helps to slow down the conversation by creating a sense of calm. Counselees sense our respect and genuine interest in hearing what they have to say.

The Importance of Responding Well

In addition to these practices of good listening, it is important that we as caregivers work to be proficient in how we speak, that we use words in ways that construct hope and possibility for change. I encourage the following as some of the elements of speaking well in counseling conversations:

Being Tentative in What We Say

From the position of not knowing, it is helpful for the counselor to frame statements in a manner that communicates respect for the counselee's expertise regarding the problem. For example, in a counseling session, when the individual has explained her experience with the problem, I offer a tentative summary of what I have heard her say. I express this tentative understanding using phrases such as, "Tell me if that sounds like I am understanding what you think is important for me to know."

Asking for Clarification

Sometimes people say something, and they know what they mean, but we may not understand. Asking counselees to clarify communicates that we are working to understand *their* perspectives. For example, imagine that a counselee says, "My life is such a mess." It will help me to understand what he is communicating by asking if he will explain "mess." And as counselees work to make it clear to me, they often come to understand it better themselves.

Using Their Metaphors

I work to stay particularly attuned to metaphors that individual counselees use because the metaphor communicates specific perspectives and emotions they have regarding situations in their lives. Consider the statement, "I feel like my life is on a merry-go-round." The metaphor of a merry-go-round suggests a routine, a same-old-thing type of outlook. It offers the potential for in-depth conversation and a way of connecting with the counselee, specifically because the counselee understands what the metaphor means. Asking her to explain a bit more about the "merry-go-round" can help us both to understand more about her experience.

Asking Open Questions

Notice the difference between asking, "Do you like your parents?" and, "Will you talk about your feelings for your parents?" The first question is a closed question, leaving room for a yes or no answer. The second question allows for a greater range of responses and, I believe, more helpful information.

Asking One Question at a Time

An important skill in asking good questions is to formulate the question well and then allow for an answer. Particularly for people who tend to think out loud, it can be challenging to formulate one clear question to ask. Consider the following question(s) to a counselee: "Will you tell me a bit about how this conversation can be helpful to you, what sorts of things you are struggling with, what is going on in your family, and what you want to work on?" Which question is the counselee supposed to answer? Should she discuss what she hopes for, what has been difficult, her family, or the reason for coming in? I work to teach the skill of formulating what we will say before we speak and then allowing time for the answer.

Giving up the Need to Say Something Clever

This injunction is often a revolutionary and paradigmatic shift for trainees who, particularly because they have been identified as gifted for this ministry of care, have assumed that their job description must entail imparting great wisdom and giving sound spiritual advice. In contrast, they learn that honoring the perspectives and strengths of another is often more empowering than offering expert solutions. They come to realize that attempting to be clever or insightful prevents them from listening well because they are busy trying to think of something brilliant to say. They also realize that the need to be clever means that rather than being helpful to the counselee, they may be focusing on meeting their own need to be appreciated or seen as wise.

With the assumptions of Solution-Focused Counseling and the basic skills of good listening and helpful conversations in mind, I now turn to a review of Solution-Focused techniques and how they can be used in a counseling session. In the counseling experiences I have had with people who honored me by inviting me into conversations regarding their difficulties, I have come to a deep appreciation for these techniques that other practitioners have developed over the years. In my experience, they offer practical tools for opening space in conversations that allows counselees to begin finding a different relationship with the burdens that bring them to counseling.

I often begin teaching the techniques with examples of contrasting conversations: an admittedly counterproductive counseling conversation, and a conversation that demonstrates the posture the Solution-Focused approach offers. As you read the following imaginary conversations with a young woman named Alice, notice the perceptions the counselor in each version seems to have about his role as the counselor for Alice, and also how each counselor seems to perceive Alice.

Alice: Trouble Maker or Normal Girl?

Alice is a fifteen-year-old, middle-class young lady whom the school administrator refers to as "uncontrollable, impulsive, and manipulative." Since entering the new school last semester, Alice has struggled to fit in with other students and has had several escalating conflicts with one particular group. The latest crisis occurred two weeks ago when a teacher had to intervene as a fight broke out between Alice and another student. Alice's parents have been encouraged to find someone to provide "anger management counseling."

Conversation A

Counselor: C

Alice: A

C: So, I understand there was a fight at school, and your parents want you to find some help for managing your anger. Can you tell me what happened?

A: It's not my fault. That girl has been asking for it for a long time. When she walks past me in the hall, she and her little friends all start laughing, and I know they're talking about me. During lunch, they all sit together and whisper and laugh, and if I look at their table, they act like they were laughing at something else. The fight in the hall started when she tried to block me from going to my locker. I said, "Excuse me," and when I walked past, she hit me in the back of the head.

C: Your parents told me the teacher who stopped the fight said that Brittany did nothing to provoke you. She said you walked over, pushed her against the locker, and started hitting her, and that three people—including the school custodian—saw the whole thing.

A: See, nobody believes me. Everybody says it's my fault. (Starting to cry and burying her head in her hands) Everybody is against me, and nobody believes me. But I'm telling you, she started it.

C: Well, it's hard to believe you when eyewitnesses claim otherwise. Don't you think you should be more honest about what happened? If you would just admit you were wrong and apologize, this could all be over by now.

A: I *am* telling you the truth. Brittany hit me. She's been asking for it for a long time. She's the one that needs counseling, but she and her little group of friends get to do anything they want.

C: That's not the story I heard. The students who saw it said that Brittany didn't even see you coming and that you shoved her from behind.

A: That's a lie! She started the fight. I'm sick of her getting away with everything and getting me in trouble.

C: Alice, you have to be honest about these things, and even if she teases you and laughs at you, that does not give you the right to attack her. Have you thought about trying to be her friend?

A: I tried being nice to her one day, and all she did was make fun of me when I walked away.

C: Well, maybe you need to just learn to ignore her?

A: It's kind of impossible to ignore someone who's blocking you from being able to open your locker. I said, "Excuse me," and when I walked past her, she hit me.

C: Alice, let's get real here. You dress in Goth clothes but get mad that people laugh at you. You've been seen smoking behind the gym, you run with the group of kids that are known for making trouble... Everything about you makes you look guilty. This counseling is not going to work if you don't try to help yourself, and you can't do that if you can't be honest and take responsibility for what you did, and for who you are.

Conversation B

Counselor: C

Alice: A

C: So, I understand there was a fight at school and your parents want you to find some help for managing your anger. I'm interested in what you think about all this and how you think our talking about it might be helpful.

A: First of all, it's not my fault. That girl has been asking for it for a long time. When she walks past me in the hall, she and her little friends all start laughing, and I know they're talking about me. During lunch, they all sit together and whisper and laugh, and if I look at their table, they act like they were laughing at something else. The fight in the hall started when she tried to block me from going to my locker. I said, "Excuse me," and when I walked past, she hit me in the back of the head.

C: I can see that this is a very frustrating situation for you. There are some things that aren't clear to me that you can probably help me understand, but what I'm interested in first is just to know how you would like for things to be at school.

A: (Irritated) What I want is to be left alone.

C: That is very interesting, and I noticed that you didn't hesitate a bit about answering my question that way. Can you say a little more about why being left alone is important to you?

A: Because I just want to be a normal person. I don't want to get into fights; I just want to go to school. I'm tired of getting pushed around.

C: I'm really sorry that being in school has been so difficult for you. So, can you tell me a little more about being left alone, and being normal?

A: Well, it's pretty hard to act normal when you feel like everyone is looking at you. That witch Brittany is always trying to get a rise out of me. She waits in front of my locker every day, just so she can mess with me.

C: So, even just walking to your locker every day makes you feel anxious?

A: I just know that the best part of her day is focused on making trouble for me.

C: That sounds very frustrating. I want to ask you a different kind of question . . . If you were being treated as a normal person and not getting into fights, what would you be doing instead?

A: Well, I could walk down the hall and not be wondering if people were laughing at me.

C: So, if you were walking down the hall and no one was laughing at you, what would you be doing?

A: I would be relaxed, not all tensed up, and I wouldn't avoid making eye contact with people.

C: I can see that you really wish that you could be different at school than how you seem to think you are perceived. Has there ever been a time when you felt a little bit normal, like you described, maybe a little more relaxed?

A: I guess I felt a little better one day when I was walking down the hall and I saw this girl from my biology class using crutches. I offered to carry her backpack, and while we were walking, she told me how she had broken her ankle skiing, and as we talked, I didn't even notice if other people were watching me.

C: What a great story. You didn't just *feel* normal; you *were* normal. What is it about you that knew how to be a friend to somebody who needed help?

The counselor in Conversation A seems to view himself as needing to convince Alice of her guilt and then offer solutions such as forgiving the other girl, making friends with her, or ignoring her. As often happens when a counselor tries to shame a counselee, Alice only became more defiant. And as is common when counselors offer their own solutions, Alice had either already tried the suggestions of her counselor or didn't believe they would help.

In Conversation B, the counselor works to come alongside Alice, to hear what she thinks about the situation, and to learn how she would like for things to be. Notice that Counselor B did not agree or disagree with Alice about her guilt. He did not even focus on the incident with the other student; rather, he asked what life would be like for Alice without the problem that led her to counseling. This is the type of conversation from which a Solution-Focused counselor seeks to work.

Techniques of Solution-Focused Counseling

As with most models of counseling, a Solution-Focused session normally begins with a time for greeting one another, helping the counselee to get comfortable, and building rapport. Following a friendly greeting and introductions, I think a good opening is to ask counselees to talk about "how they think having this conversation can be helpful." As they begin to explain the difficulties that have led to this moment, our primary goal is to seek to understand *how they understand* their experience. I believe that one thing people value the most in good counseling is the simple fact that someone attentively listened to them and worked to understand what they were going through. People often just need to vent, to be allowed to express their frustration, to be able to cry, to express their pain or anger, even to express their hopelessness.

An agenda with no other purpose than to be an empathic presence is an unselfish gift of care.

Of course, while people need and deeply value someone who will listen and allow them to vent, I also know that they often want more from us. They want help working through their difficulties and finding ways to change the destructive patterns in their lives. My own style of working with people is to allow them all the time they need to vent. After that space is opened and they are given the opportunity to express what they need, people will often give some type of signal that indicates they are finished and ready to move on. They may say something like, "That about sums it all up." At that point in the conversation, I believe it is helpful to draw from the techniques of the Solution-Focused approach.

I begin this presentation of the techniques of Solution-Focused Counseling with the important proviso that these are tools that practitioners of the model have found useful, but they are only that: tools. Good listening, expressions of empathy, and simply the fact that the counselor cares about the counselee are certainly more important than any technique we might use.

The Miracle Question

Many consider the Miracle Question the hallmark technique of the Solution-Focused model. I have used it often to help shift the conversation away from the problem and toward a solution. When the counselee has had time to vent, and she affirms that I understand the problem *as she wants me to*, my typical next step is to give a brief summary of what I have heard, along with a message of empathy. For example, a more complete conversation with Alice would allow her to talk more about her frustrations, to neither absolve nor convict her, but to understand what her experience and perspective are and to be an empathic presence for her. At some point, I would summarize my understanding of her condition and ask if she feels that I have heard what is important for her. If she confirms that I have, I would ask the Miracle Question:

I'm going to ask you an unusual question that is often very helpful to people, so take your time. Imagine that tonight when you go to bed, all the problems that we've talked about are still on your mind, still with you . . . and then tomorrow morning, you wake up, and you have some sense that a miracle has occurred. All the problems you've described are in the past, and your day at school is what you want it to be. As you think about that miracle, what will you notice that tells you it has happened?

The theory behind the Miracle Question is that difficulties in our lives can be so pervasive that, as a problem occupies our mind, we focus only on it, rather than on a solution. The weight of the problem and the attention we give it make it difficult to imagine life without it. Envisioning the miracle engenders hope and turns toward the solution rather than the problem. It also helps the counselor to understand what counselees want, rather than just what they don't want.

The counselor might not always frame the question as a "miracle" specifically. What is important to recognize is that some form of a question that explores what the counselee's life will be like without the problem helps to move the conversation away from the problem and toward the solution. In Conversation B, Alice's counselor used a version of the Miracle Question: "How would you like for things to be at school?" At that point, the conversation changed from Alice as a troublemaker to what Alice would be like without the problem.

Focusing on Strengths

Consistent with the Solution-Focused assumption that people have the resources they need to solve their problems, it is helpful to identify and emphasize strength and resilience in the counselee. Affirming what he does well and acknowledging any perseverance that we notice in the counselee helps to engender hope and encourages responsibility for his life. In Conversation A, Alice's counselor communicated a judgmental, condescending opinion toward her that reinforced her defensiveness and resistance. In contrast, Counselor B, without making excuses for her, maintained an affirming presence with Alice. He drew the focus away from what might be weakness, toward strength—for instance, pointing out that Alice "knew how to be a friend" to the girl with crutches. This focus on counselee strengths offers an important perspective for the Solution-Focused counselor in all of the techniques that follow.

Exception-Building

Solution-Focused counselors often follow the Miracle Question by asking the counselee if she has ever experienced even just a bit of the miracle (or difference) she describes. In Conversation B, Alice stated that she just wanted to be a "normal person," and the counselor asked, "Has there ever been a time when you felt a little bit normal, like you described?" Alice then told about helping the girl with crutches. That action was an "exception" to the problem of her not feeling normal. From the identification of that one simple exception, Alice and the counselor could work to expand on that difference. The counselor next asked, "What is it about you that knew how to be a friend to somebody that needed help?"

Although this imagined conversation ends at that point, the counselor would continue to expand on the exception that Alice identified. For example, the counselor might say, "When you were helping the girl with the crutches, you said that you didn't even notice if other people were watching you. As you remember that experience, are there other things you didn't notice?" Or the counselor could ask, "When are some other times you didn't notice people watching you?" or, "When you don't feel like you are being watched, what feelings do you notice instead?" or, "What thoughts were going through your mind since you didn't feel noticed?" The intention behind this line of questioning is to detail the "miracle" as much as possible, and to introduce small steps that make up the desired solution.

Imaging the Solution

Another technique that is helpful in building solutions is to ask the counselee to "see" and "hear" the differences before and after the miracle. The counselor would say to Alice, "Imagine that we have two videotapes: one of you when 'not-normal' is in control, and one when 'normal' is at work. If we turn the sound off, what are some things you will see that help you know which of the videos you are watching?" He might also ask, "What might other people notice that would help them distinguish the two tapes?" or, "If we turn the sound on and the picture off, what will you or others hear that is different in the two versions?"

Scaling Questions

People who are overwhelmed with a problem in their life often see the problem in an all-or-nothing frame of reference, but based on the assumption that exceptions can be found to every problem, the counselor works to introduce the possibility of even a small hint of difference. Scaling questions can help people discover those exceptions. As a trainee once shared in a supervisory session, "I love scaling questions because they let the counselee see that things can be better. Scaling normalizes what they are going through and can give them a steady diet of small choices."

Explaining the usefulness of scaling questions, Frank N. Thomas and Jack Cockburn state, "An important assumption in this regard is that every complaint description includes some sort of exception . . . nothing happens 100 percent of the time. Change is often easier both to conceptualize and to achieve when it is removed from the all or nothing dichotomy."[8] In asking scaling questions, the counselor uses the language and metaphors of the counselee to structure a scale of the individual's relationship with his problem. For example, the counselor could say to Alice:

---

8. Thomas and Cockburn, *Competency Based Counseling*, 68, 49.

> I'd like for you to think of a continuum from zero to ten, with zero representing the lowest point on the scale. At zero, you are so far from natural and from not being noticed that you feel like Brittany and those other girls must have dropped their classes just to follow your every step and give you a hard time. At the opposite extreme, ten represents a point beyond your expectations. You could be voted Most Popular Student of the Century. Where would you say you are on the scale?

Note that in this scale, I worked to create opposite extreme positions. I think it is helpful to create the scale at even ridiculous extremes for two reasons. First, in my experience, when counselees hear the extreme zero, they realize that perhaps their problem could be worse. Second, the extremes help to deconstruct the all-or-nothing dichotomy that is so common, and we can then help them to recognize small steps they can begin to take toward managing the problem.

Using the answer the counselee gives for the scale, the counselor can then structure a variety of exception-finding questions. For example: "You say you are at a four on this scale. Where will you be on the scale when you are able to say that our work together has accomplished what you hope it will?" or, "You say that you are at a four on this scale. If you saw yourself at a five, what would be different? What would you notice first?"

Any number of questions and practices can be formulated using the scaling technique. I've found that it is useful to measure progress at the end of a session by offering a scale and asking counselees where they are as a result of the conversation we've just had. I've used scaling questions to ask counselees where they would like to be on the scale, and then to ask how they will know when they are there. I've used scaling questions to ask where they would like to be on the scale when they return for our next session, and then in the next session, I ask them where they are, or where they were during the last week.

Coping Questions

There are occasionally instances when a counselee ranks herself at a zero on the scale, explaining that the problem is at its absolute worst. A good first response is usually one of empathy: "I'm sorry to hear that things are being so difficult." Working carefully to not sound like we are discounting the difficulty, coping questions can engender hope even in the worst of times. A counselor might say, "I'm sorry that is being so difficult for you. I'm also impressed that even though the problem is as bad as it is, you still managed to come to counseling, and you seem to believe that things can be better. Can you talk about where you think that strength comes from?" Another coping question could be, "It sounds like the problem is working hard to bring you down. How do you think you managed to at least keep it from being even worse?"

These are only some of the techniques that practitioners of a Solution-Focused approach to counseling have developed. I emphasize to trainees that they will be effective as they adapt these tools to their own developing styles of caregiving. While I think it is important to remain consistent with the assumptions of Solution-Focused counseling, the presentation of these techniques is not meant to be prescriptive. As a teacher of these ideas, I always enjoy observing trainees as they begin to discover what fits for them. And I have particularly enjoyed seeing how those who use these concepts find ways to add their own creative tools in helping conversations. I encourage that same creative freedom for any readers who may someday use this book in helping others to have good conversations.

5

Protecting Those in Our Care

*Ethical Guidelines for Lay Caregivers
and the Church*

Primum non nocere—Latin for, "Above all, do no harm"—is assumed to be at least implicit in the Hippocratic Oath used in medical ethics. This guiding principle for physicians holds that the patient's well being is always the primary concern in giving care. Certainly, it is reasonable to expect nothing less from those who give spiritual and mental care. Academic programs that train licensed counselors routinely require that students be instructed in the codes and parameters of ethical practices of counseling, which are oriented toward protecting both the counselee and the counselor.[1] When counseling students complete their training and seek licensure, the required exam rigorously tests their understanding of the ethical code endorsed by the licensing organization. Once licensed, the counselor in practice is required to sign an annual commitment to the code of ethics, as well as to complete regular Continuing Education Units (CEUs) in ethical practice.

While the ministry of volunteer pastoral caregiving does not offer the same level of authoritative regulation, I firmly believe that it is essential for churches to establish a process of ethical instruction, continuing dialogue, supervision, and ongoing confirmation

---

1. The Council for Accreditation of Counseling and Related Educational Programs (CACREP) identifies professional orientation and ethical practice as one of the eight core curricular experiences to be included in counselor preparation programs. See Council for Accreditation of Counseling & Related Educational Programs, http://www.cacrep.org.

of ethical adherence and ethical understanding for those who offer pastoral care. This ethical commitment must begin with congregational leaders and pastoral care staff, and it should extend to all volunteer caregivers in the church.

Ethical Concerns for Caregivers

It is interesting to note that while the contemporary professional workplace, and particularly the "helping" vocations, have propagated the need for systemizing standards of ethical behavior, many churches and ministers have generally not followed the same pattern. A 2012 survey of leaders of The National Association of Evangelicals reported that "71 percent of evangelical leaders are not required to sign a formal code of ethics."[2] Paul Camenisch explains, "One reason the clergy has been slower than the other major professions to develop its own distinctive ethic is that this atypical moral commitment was assumed to be so central to the profession that many thought it insulting to suggest that specific rules and guidelines were needed to require it."[3]

In contrast, marriage and family therapist and ethicist Gregory Brock believes that "of all the helping professions 'clergy counselors' have the greatest risk of being confronted with ethical dilemmas."[4] His reasons for concern include the realities that most theological training focuses on intellectual formation, rather than character formation; that theological training tends to give less attention to unresolved personal issues than counseling training; and that theological training often emphasizes the mind and the spirit, rather than the body and sexuality. While some of these items may not particularly be the experience of the volunteer counselor, who has probably not been theologically trained,

---

2. Murashko, "Pastors Urged to Sign Newly Released Code of Ethics,"
https://www.christianpost.com/news/pastors-urged-to-sign-newly-released-code-of-ethics.html.

3. Camenisch, "Clergy Ethics and the Professional Ethics Model," 125.

4. Brock, *American Association for Marriage and Family Therapy Ethics Casebook*, 157.

other items of concern for Brock certainly pertain to both clergy and volunteer caregivers.

Personal Issues

A first concern is that there may be issues in the volunteer's own life that, unless resolved, can be problematic in caring for others. The close supervision of lay counseling programs that I envision will hopefully ensure that when these issues are problematic in a volunteer's life, he will be guided toward someone who can help him work through these concerns. In my own counseling training, it was not uncommon for students in the program to be expected to consult with a counselor for help with their personal issues before continuing their studies.

Transference and Counter-Transference

Brock also raises concern about the "adulation"[5] that members of the congregation sometimes have for their minister. As representatives of God, and because they are often seen as and expected to be models of Christian character, it is common for ministers or volunteer caregivers to appear to have their lives together, especially in the view of people with broken lives. In counseling terms, this idea is expressed as "transference": the counselee unconsciously projects onto the counselor the unresolved issues she has with past authority figures. For example, a counselee who grew up with an overbearing father may transfer the feelings that relationship created into the relationship with her counselor. Coupled with a view of the caregiver as a representative of God, the issue of transference can become particularly problematic.

The term "counter-transference" is used to identify the opposite direction of transference, in which a counselor may project onto the counselee from his unresolved issues. For example, a

---

5. Brock, *American Association for Marriage and Family Therapy Ethics Casebook*, 161.

counselor raised by a father who was abusive may project unresolved feelings from that relationship onto the counselee. Sound ethical teaching on the challenges and management of transference and counter-transference can help caregivers to maintain healthy boundaries with those in our care.

Serving Ourselves through Our Caregiving

Another concern for Brock that applies to both vocational ministers and volunteers is that availability, compassion, and empathy are, in essence, qualities that the congregation expects from its minister.[6] Most volunteer caregivers enter into that ministry specifically because they feel they have the gift for extending empathy and compassion. While those qualities are important to the expression of good caregiving, their expression can be problematic if not managed from an ethical framework. It certainly feels good to have someone in need of our help, but if our motivation is grounded in the need to have our own self-esteem bolstered by being helpful, we are serving ourselves rather than those in our care. Appropriate touch, honoring the privacy of the care recipient, and protecting the boundaries of a counseling relationship are essential practices for both ministers and volunteers.

The confidentiality principle of counseling is also a concern for Brock in regard to clergy and volunteers.[7] Referred to as the "priest-penitent privilege," this core value of counseling ethics should certainly be of paramount concern for the lay caregiver. In principle, the value states that caregivers do not reveal confidential information about individuals in their care to anyone, unless the information involves potential harm or danger to someone.

---

6. Brock, *American Association for Marriage and Family Therapy Ethics Casebook*, 160.

7. Brock, *American Association for Marriage and Family Therapy Ethics Casebook*, 159.

Confidentiality

According to Miriam Stock Parent, "Violations of confidentiality are the most common boundary violation of clergy or counselor. These violations come as a result of several issues: duty to report, dual relationships, and undefined boundaries."[8] It is important to stress that the ultimate intention of the priest-penitent privilege is protection of the counselee. Far too many instances of the violation of confidentiality occur—not just in failing to protect a confidence, but also when the unethical behavior of a counselor or minister is hidden behind the veil of privilege to protect the perpetrator or the church.

Dual Relationships

A final ethical concern that Brock raises for clergy, and also a prime issue for volunteer caregivers, is how to manage dual relationships. As Richard Gula explains, dual relationships occur in pastoral care "when we interact with another person in more than one capacity."[9] In professional counseling, dual relationships are forbidden. Licensed counselors do not accept family members, friends, or romantic interests as clients. For ministers and lay caregivers, this distinction, by the very nature of the caregiving role, is less precise. A minster is both pastor and friend to the individuals in her church. A lay caregiver is a member of her church along with those who receive her care. When managed well, the dynamics of these dual relationships actually offer the opportunity to be helpful. From an ecclesiological perspective, our role as fellow Christians is to bear the burdens of others. Thus, the reality of dual relationships for the lay counselor offers both the potential for meaningful care and the danger of ethical compromise. Counselors must manage this dichotomy from within the boundaries of the core principle of counseling ethics: "Above all, do no harm."

---

8. Parent, "Boundaries and Roles in Ministry Counseling," 1–25.
9. Gula, *Ethics in Pastoral Ministry*, 80.

Accountability

With these principles in mind, it is also essential to maintain measures of accountability. Compared to the structures in place for licensed counselors—an ethical board reviews and reports charges of unethical behavior—there is a lamentable isolation from any kind of accountability system for many ministers, particularly those in standalone, free-church traditions. I recommend that lay caregiving programs in the church, under the guidance of a knowledgeable lawyer, adopt a system similar to those found in the ethical codes of professional counseling. Further, I encourage individual ministers in small congregations, who are often the only staff members to work with local ministerial alliances, to forge relationships and commitments to ethical practice and accountability.

Having reviewed the potential pitfalls that counselors face, it is important to discuss the steps that counselors *should* be taking. What follows is a rationale and delineation of ethical standards for lay caregivers. I have framed this conversation in an ecclesiological context that seeks to understand the ethical implications of power in the counseling relationship, as well as the ethical principles that arise from an understanding of power.

An Ecclesiological Perspective of Ethical Caregiving

The assumption that pastoral caregiving is first and foremost a theological task is grounded in an ecclesiological perspective that pastoral care is the responsibility and privilege of the community of Christians, who are called to bear one another's burdens. In the timeless words of theologian Dietrich Bonhoeffer, "[T]he ministry of listening has been committed to them by Him who is Himself the great listener and whose work they should share. We should listen with the ears of God that we may speak the Word of God."[10]

---

10. Bonhoeffer, *Life Together*, 98–99.

Paul clearly speaks of this call to bear the burdens of others in his letter to the Galatians:

> Bear one another's burdens, and in this way you will fulfill the law of Christ. For if those who are nothing think they are something, they deceive themselves. All must test their own work; then that work, rather than their neighbor's work, will become a cause for pride. For all must carry their own loads.[11]

The attentive reader may observe something of a contradiction in this text between verse 2—"Bear one another's burdens"—and verse 5—"For all must carry their own loads." Which is it? Are we to help one another or not? In modern colloquial terms, if others depend on us, are we being "codependent?" As explained in Vine's New Testament Greek Dictionary, "The difference between *baros* (burden in verse 2) and *phortion* in verse 5 is, that *baros* always suggests what is 'heavy or burdensome' while *phortion* is simply 'something to be borne,' without reference to its weight."[12] It seems then that the Galatians passage actually suggests a distinction in the levels of help that we give to others. The text recognizes that some burdens are simply too heavy to bear alone; there are also burdens so light that two people carrying them together actually makes no sense. Think of moving a piano. One person could not manage the weight and size of this object on his own. Compare that image to a backpack, a load intentionally designed for one person to carry and rather awkward for two. This seeming contradiction in Galatians is actually instructive to the conversation of counseling ethics. As the caregiver works to appropriately support those in his care, helping to lift the burdens of life that cannot be endured alone, he also allows the troubled individual to manage the load that is her own responsibility.

Therefore, the ecclesiological perspective undergirding this discussion is the call to bear the burdens of others as they also carry what is theirs alone. With this perspective, we move to an

---

11. Galatians 6:2–5.

12. Vine's Greek New Testament Dictionary, http://gospelhall.org/bible/bible.php?search=phortion&dict=vine&lang=greek.

overview of basic ethical guidelines. It should become evident through the discussion of these guidelines that they provide a practical structure that will help the caregiver manage this balance between being helpful and being overly responsible.

Essential Principles of Ethical Caregiving

In *Just Ministry: Professional Ethics for Pastoral Ministers*, one of the more instructive books on ethics for pastors, Richard Gula offers his perspective on pastoral care and ethical responsibility—a perspective that also applies well to the role of the lay caregiver.[13] In particular, Gula raises the issues of power and confidentiality, which are fundamental principles of many ethical codes in the field of counseling.

An Ethical Understanding of Power

When an individual, couple, or family arrives for a conversation with a person who has been identified as having expertise in helping others, a relationship is immediately established in which certain power dynamics are present. People who seek help from others sense a lack of their own expertise to manage a problem that is often overwhelming to them. In similar fashion, when a patient consults a medical doctor with a physical problem, he expects the physician to have the training and expertise he needs. Because the doctor has the knowledge to perhaps offer appropriate treatment, the patient is invested in a relationship of depending on that doctor to use his knowledge as a medical authority in a beneficial way. Gula observes, "When some form of public validation legitimates our personal power, we speak of having 'authority.'"[14] Therefore, an understanding of the principles of ethical caregiving must begin with a clear perspective of the power that is implicit in a helping relationship.

13. Gula, *Just Ministry*.
14. Gula, *Just Ministry*, 123.

The Power of Expertise

The work of French philosopher Michel Foucault has had a significant impact on the discussion of power, knowledge, and ethics in the practice of marriage and family therapy. In his masterful work *Discipline and Punish: The Birth of the Prison*, Foucault describes the reinforcing nature of power and knowledge and how the process between them functions to maintain authority. To illustrate how power is defined and implemented in society, Foucault refers to London social reformer Jeremy Bentham's proposal for a modernized prison. In his proposal, the prison would be housed in an architectural structure he called the "Panopticon."[15] Bentham envisioned this prison as a circular structure of individual, side-by-side cells with windows facing the guard's tower in the center. Although the technology did not yet exist, Bentham imagined the structure as having "one-way" windows, which guards could see through, but prisoners could not. Bentham's proposal was that the prisoner, with no way of knowing when and if the unseen guards were scrutinizing him, would always abide by the rules of the prison. With the threat of knowledge of each prisoner's cell, the guards would not only maintain power over each prisoner's behavior, they would also have the power to define what proper behavior was.

Foucault believed that, like the watchful eye of the prison guard, the power structures of culture function to determine the values, expectations, and behaviors of a society, and in determining those norms, also evaluate the success or failure of each citizen's performance. On living within this power structure, Foucault says, "In the end we are judged, condemned, classified, determined in our undertaking, destined to a certain mode of living or dying, as a function of the true discourses which are the bearers of the specific effects of power."[16]

---

15. Foucault, *Power/Knowledge*, 94.
16. Foucault, *Power/Knowledge*, 94.

The Power and Responsibility of Representing the Church

These ideas offer an important perspective for ministry and counseling. As representatives of the church, we also represent the discourses of the church. When people come to us and reveal their struggles, it is reasonable to assume they are also wondering how they are being seen. Do we think they are crazy? That they are a lost cause? Do we think they are bad or incompetent people? Do they measure up to the expectations they think we have for them? As they open their lives to us, they also want us to think well of them. As representatives of the church, people see us as examples of what "good" Christians should be like. We have the power to define what proper behavior is. Like prisoners under scrutiny in the Panopticon, people in our care are often unsure of what we are looking at, but they are constantly measuring themselves by what they think we might expect.

In addition to representing the discourse of the church, as counselors we also represent the cultural discourse of mental health. As discussed in the third chapter of this work, the language of psychology has been absorbed into our culture as a primary resource for managing life's most difficult problems, and for establishing the expectations of what it means to be mentally healthy. In *Saving the Modern Soul*, Eva Illouz explains that counseling conversations take place within a socially constructed process in which "the self is made to work seamlessly for and within a system of power."[17] She adds that the "modern therapeutic discourse has been incorporated into different institutional settings such as the corporation, the family, and ordinary practices of self-help."[18] Illouz further proposes that the influence of psychology has transformed our modern understanding of life's difficulties and suffering from the earlier religious perspective to the current secularized frame. In her article "How Therapy Became a Multimillion Dollar Industry," she adds:

---

17. Illouz, *Saving the Modern Soul*, 3.
18. Illouz, *Saving the Modern Soul*, 7.

> Human beings have long suffered from afflictions of the soul, but how we conceived of them in the past was very different from how we define them today. Afflictions of the soul were understood in religious terms... We now think of afflictions of the soul in psychological terms, as originating in a childhood conflict or trauma, and believe they can improve by talking about them and changing our interpretations of ourselves and others. Psychologists have redefined the psyche and their power has had important political consequences... No social group in the 20th century has been as ubiquitous as the psychologists, as they redefined the nature of human motivation, conflict, and harmony.[19]

For the pastoral caregiver, it is important to consider how the worldview of psychology has constructed the expectations and approaches for dealing with problems, even within the church. As I stated in chapter 3, "Our society and many times our churches are enamored by the claim that life's most difficult problems call for psychological treatment." This worldview, shaped in the psychology of our culture, is entrusted to the minister as well as the lay pastoral caregiver when offering a ministry of care and counsel.

We find ourselves, therefore, in a dual role: we extend psychological care, and we also function as representatives of the church—and even as representatives of God. This combination imbues us with enormous and potentially dangerous authority in people's lives. One need only think of the many horrendous cases of sexual abuse by Catholic priests to understand the tragedy of abusing that power. Gula discusses the symbolic representation in our role as caregiver:

> We bring "something more" to ministry than just ourselves... [W]e are for people representatives of the sacred. We represent a community of faith, a religious tradition, a way of life, and, yes, even God. Some people feel that

---

19. Illouz, "How Therapy Became a Multimillion Dollar Industry," http://www.haaretz.com/israel-news/how-therapy-became-a-multimillion-dollar-industry-1.436431.

to talk with us is to talk with God, or to be accepted or rejected by us is to be accepted or rejected by God.[20]

Managing the power of our role requires both theological understanding and ethical praxis. Chapter 2 of this work offered a brief treatment of a theological perspective on Solution-Focused Counseling, but theoretical concepts on their own are inadequate. Ethical practice also requires that a genuine personal commitment guide our relationships with those in our care. The weight of this responsibility—having expertise in counseling while also representing God, and bearing the authority of God and society in the lives of those in our care—is a gift that, managed well, can be a great blessing, but when abused or mishandled, can cause untold damage.

Managing this authority well begins, as Gula says, with an acceptance of the fact that "[t]he greater burden of moral responsibility falls on the one with the greater power."[21] Recognizing and managing this burden must be grounded in the lay caregiver's commitment to first set aside his own desires and needs, and then to accept the position of one who has the greater responsibility.

Considerations for Dual Relationships

In his discussion, Gula raises a particularly important ethical issue for the volunteer caregiver who, not formally on the church staff, may consider herself "less-official"—just another church member. As just another church member, she may see herself simply as a friend. Gula refers to this common perspective as the "lure of the friendship model." He explains that "trying to make the pastoral relationship a peer relationship only falsifies its real nature and puts us at greater risk of unethical behavior."[22] In the church, we are certainly equal as Christians, but we are not equal when given the role of representatives of the church. As a paid minister or volunteer,

---

20. Gula, *Just Ministry*, 30.
21. Gula, *Just Ministry*, 133.
22. Gula, *Ethics in Pastoral Ministry*, 76.

the designation of representative assigns a certain distinction of power and authority within the community. The act of seeking help to manage the burdens of life from an individual appointed by the church requires a certain measure of vulnerability. This, in turn, brings the expectation that the caregiver is entrusted with power extending beyond mere friendship. Managing that power differential requires cautious awareness that when a church member serves as volunteer caregiver or church representative for another member of the church, a dual relationship exists.

A dual relationship like this inevitably has an impact on the friendship in question. To this end, author Martha Ellen Stortz offers an instructive perspective. She encourages an awareness of how representing the church distinguishes these "equal in Christ" relationships, and she details seven important factors to consider.[23]

Consideration #1: Choice

Stortz observes that in friendship, there is an element of "choice."[24] In equal relationships, both parties have the freedom to determine whether they want to become friends. In the commitment of ministry, however, that choice is not ours to make. We extend our pastoral care to those in need, regardless of our personal preferences for the types of people with whom we prefer to spend our time.

Consideration #2: Personal Needs

Next, she explains that friendships are typically formed by similarity of shared interests[25]—things that both parties like or dislike, agree or disagree about. However, in ministry, the focus toward those in our care is helping the other while suspending our personal needs from the conversation. Certainly, connection is valuable, and I teach the necessity of building rapport when beginning a counseling conversation. But the focus in pastoral caregiving is

---

23. Stortz, *PastorPower*, 111–17.
24. Stortz, *PastorPower*, 111.
25. Stortz, *PastorPower*, 112–13.

helping the other be comfortable and striving to understand his life experiences and view of the world. Rapport may deepen our connection with the one in need, but the purpose of that connection is to be helpful to the other.

Consideration #3: Judgment

In friendship, we also have an affinity of interests, values, and common goals, and this is Stortz's third point for readers to consider. As members of a church, we share what we consider to be the ultimate values and goals of life with others in our fellowship of faith. But often, in a caregiving relationship, the person reaching out to us for help may hold a view of her particular story that is very different from ours. Suspending judgment is an important but sometimes difficult caregiving skill, particularly when someone reveals a perspective that we find immoral or contrary to our values. I do believe that there are instances when the authority of pastoral correction is called for, but those comments are often counterproductive to the relationship and to the possibility that the individual will feel sufficiently accepted until we have developed a trusting relationship.

Consideration #4: Equality

Stortz puts it simply: "Friends share equal power and status."[26] As stated earlier, we are equal in our status as Christians, but as representatives of the church, we have the greater power in the caregiving relationship.

Consideration #5: Reciprocity

Another concern for Stortz is "reciprocity."[27] Over time, an equal back-and-forth sharing takes place in friendships between two people, and this exchange is a great blessing. As caregivers, we are

---

26. Stortz, *PastorPower*, 114.
27. Stortz, *PastorPower*, 115.

often truly blessed by those with whom we work, but our task is to be a blessing to them. To expect reciprocal benefit from the other is a violation of our power.

Consideration #6: Knowledge

Stortz points out that friends "invite equal self-disclosure."[28] A shared vulnerability characterizes good friendships; we often confide things to our friends that we carefully protect from those with whom we don't have such a trusting relationship. The pastoral caregiving relationship is one in which others come to us in vulnerability, frequently confiding things about their lives that they would not share with anyone else. Because they come to us for care, we provide a level of trust that makes such openness a possibility, but we do not, in turn, confide in them or seek their help with our problems. Our focus is on helping them.

The concept of knowledge as a factor of self-disclosure in friendship needs a bit more explanation. Trainees in counseling often ask, "Is it okay to tell a personal story?" My answer depends on three concerns. First: "Are you telling the story because *you* need to tell it, or because it may be helpful to the other?" If you need to tell the story because it's something you're working on in your own life, you may need to see a counselor yourself, but we don't put the counselee in that role. Second: "Are you being a good listener, or are you 'in your head,' thinking about your own life and problems as the story you want to tell comes to mind?" And third: "By giving the counselee something from your own experience, are you trying to provide him with *your* solution, or will the story help the counselee find his?" I don't think that any of this prohibits sharing from our own experience, but when our focus in the conversation is on ourselves rather than helping the other, we are not giving the best pastoral care. In any counseling I provide, I remain very tentative about sharing a story from my own life that seems similar to the counselee's; I know that even if it sounds like the exact same problem, it never is. Even if the details are precisely identical in every

---

28. Stortz, *PastorPower*, 115.

way, I faced the problem as myself, not as the counselee. I have not experienced the problem through her eyes.

The one reason I would consider sharing my own story is if doing so might "normalize" the counselee's situation. If I have honestly experienced a similar difficulty, it might be helpful for him to know that he's not completely alone—and that the difficulty can be survived. Even then, I would be cautious about suggesting, "I know what you're going through," or, "What worked for me will work for you."

Consideration #7: Benevolence

Returning to Stortz's insights, it is important to discuss one more facet of friendship. This is not a facet that we should avoid; rather, it is a beneficial dynamic in the pastoral care relationship: "Benevolence."[29] Stortz believes that "benevolence is the ability to say finally: 'I love you, not because I need you, nor because you need me, but because you are.'"[30] Gula provides his commentary on Stortz's list of the factors of friendship to consider. He observes that ministry "correlates easily with benevolence, in the sense of acting in service to our neighbor."[31] As caregivers, we seek to extend care and service for others and to act on their behalf. Again, I remind the reader that as caregivers, we don't expect reciprocal care or benevolence from the other. We don't expect to gain from the relationship.

The Continuum of Dual Relationships

In his commentary on Stortz's insights, Gula adds that it is helpful to understand the dual relationships within pastoral care on a continuum. On one end is the extreme of "professional relationship of the pastoral minister." The opposite extreme would be "intimate

---

29. Stortz, *PastorPower*, 115.
30. Stortz, *PastorPower*, 115.
31. Gula, *Just Ministry*, 134.

friend." "Friendship" lies in the middle.[32] As we move from an emphasis on the professional relationship toward intimacy, we gradually "compromise our professional commitment to the other."[33] When we become friends, we have moved out of a professional relationship into a personal one.

On occasion, I find myself seeking to manage this continuum in my own professional role as both professor and friend to students and alumni. In my free time, I enjoy playing golf, a hobby that I share with some students. Thus, I have a dual relationship as professor and golf partner. I hope I manage the continuum of this dual relationship well as I consciously work to maintain healthy boundaries between the two roles, relaxing the strictly professional function of professor but avoiding a more in-depth level of intimacy. On the golf course, we may talk about class or school, but I don't discuss the professional aspects of grading, the individual work of any students, or other elements of my authoritative role as professor. In the classroom, I consciously return to the role of professor, avoiding discussions about our golf game or suggesting that I have a special relationship with golfers in the classroom. And I work to give all my students—not just the golfers—opportunities for relationships outside of the classroom by hosting students in my family's home for dinner, eating lunch in the student lounge, and spending time with them in other more casual settings.

We must be aware that dual relationships *always* involve the risk of unethical behavior. The possibility always exists of compromising the inherent power of the one with the most authority. As professor, I have the power and authority of grading, advising, and teaching students, but on the golf course, we are equals. I believe, however, that the benefits of this equality outweigh the potential downfalls. Playing golf and enjoying other social occasions gives me and my students the opportunity to know one another and build relationships in ways that make the work we do together in the classroom more valuable to all. In the same

---

32. Gula, *Just Ministry*, 136.
33. Gula, *Just Ministry*, 136.

way, I think that in the context of ministry, the risks of dual relationships—when we manage them carefully—are outweighed by the opportunities they present.

There are certain warning signs that a counselor is failing to manage the risks of a dual relationship within the perspective of the continuum. One such indication is when we feel we must keep some aspect of our relationships a secret. Of course, our most intimate relationships certainly have aspects in which we necessarily maintain complete privacy. I share an intimate relationship with my wife, but it's not a secret that we are married. If we go away for a weekend or have dinner together, we don't try to keep those meetings unknown. And, although far less intimate, it is no secret that I play golf with students. In contrast, secret relationships are often hidden out of fear of discovery. Such relationships usually contain something that could potentially be harmful.

Admittedly, there is a risk that we will compromise one or the other extreme when entering into this continuum from professional to intimate. However, as I've experienced in these relationships with students, there is also great value. Students have an opportunity to know me in a way that I hope enriches their lives; in turn, knowing them enriches mine. I believe that the same blessings are made possible in ministry, and we certainly should not avoid them.

In contrast, the ethics of counseling forbid any type of compromise in dual relationships. As a counselor in private practice, I never developed friendships with clients. In fact, I would even inform them that if we happened to meet in public, protecting their privacy included not revealing that I knew them. If they wanted to greet me, that was fine, but the initiative was theirs. In ministry, on the other hand, our relationship with congregational members also means that they are friends. When I meet a congregational member in public, not greeting him could be viewed as an insult. Within that relationship, therefore, we don't guard the counselee's identity as a counselor would for a client. At the same time, the ethical pastor will not publicly mention something that a congregational member discussed in the privacy of counseling, nor will the ethical pastor even reveal the identities of those whom she counsels. Still, she certainly does not hide the fact that she offers pastoral care.

Good ministry is all about relationships. Many times, those relationships bring our vocational roles into social contexts. We spend our time with people professionally, but also as friends. Ministry that is built on sound ethical behavior manages that dual aspect of our role with open vulnerability and honest integrity, and such ministry seeks always to avoid compromise that may lead to reproach.

Final Words

IN THE PREFACE OF this work, I briefly referenced Howard Stone's article "The Congregational Setting of Pastoral Counseling: A Study of Pastoral Counseling Theorists from 1949–1999." In the article, Stone discusses his content analysis of literature in the field of pastoral counseling in the latter half of the twentieth century. Analyzing this literature led him to conclude that much of what is written is out of touch with the postmodern approaches that are available to the pastoral caregiver.

For instance, Stone concludes that the literature reveals a "significant long-term therapy bias . . . even when written for pastors in the congregational context who primarily do short-term counseling."[1] Stone's analysis concludes before the start of the twenty-first century; however, for the past twenty years, I have taught pastoral care to seminary students and regularly sought literature and resources that will be helpful for ministry. From this experience, I've seen no significant change—even in the current literature—from Stone's analysis. Stone also observes, "Most of the pastoral counseling theorists studied either fail to demonstrate a good grasp of the kind of counseling that occurs in parish ministry, or they show little interest in it. Many seem more in tune with classical theology, psychotherapy, or specialized pastoral counseling than with the counseling that happens in local congregations."[2]

---

1. Stone, "Congregational Setting of Pastoral Counseling," 184.
2. Stone, "Congregational Setting of Pastoral Counseling," 187.

FINAL WORDS

This book has been one small effort to contribute to the body of literature that Stone finds lacking. My hope is that it will serve as a practical resource for pastors, congregations, and ministry group leaders who either provide pastoral care or oversee those who do.

I have previously presented the content of this book in a variety of settings that are most closely aligned to parish ministry. In the process of interacting with students and others who have been through this training, I frequently see them grasp the usefulness of these ideas. This confirms for me that the Solution-Focused model *does apply* to "the counseling that happens in local congregations,"[3] as Stone describes it.

Several years ago, I had the privilege of returning to a congregation where I had implemented this model and where a group of lay caregivers were actively using their training. During that visit, I had the chance to spend time observing their ongoing ministry. I was also able to interview them about the work they were doing—particularly how they were using the Solution-Focused model.[4] From that experience, I have found it helpful when I teach these materials to regularly end classes and workshops with a period of feedback from the participants regarding our work together. I shaped these conversations with a Solution-Focused approach, asking participants a version of the Miracle Question such as, "Now that this training period is over, if you were to enter into a conversation as the counselor and, at the end of that time, feel that you did the best work you possibly could, how would you recognize that?"

With sincere gratitude to those who have taught me from their feedback, I bring this work to a close by discussing some of what I have learned from these conversations:

---

3. Stone, "Congregational Setting of Pastoral Counseling," 187.
4. Holland, "Constructing Helpful Conversations."

FINAL WORDS

Emphasize that the Counselee Is the Expert on His/Her Problem

A first lesson for me has been that trainees value the Solution-Focused assumption that "the counselee is the expert on his/her problem." Participants regularly stress the helpfulness of this idea. As one trainee explained, "I don't have any anxiety about being inept at this task; it is not our job to fix the problem."[5] Another wisely observed that using this models means "I don't have to be a detective, solving the person's problem."[6]

I have occasionally observed a difference around this assumption between seminary students preparing for church leadership and the lay members of a congregation who have been asked to serve in this ministry. The seminary students often assume that it is somehow part of their job to be able to say something that is spiritually wise, insightful, and clever. While lay members are typically relieved that they don't have to be experts, some seminary students wonder if this assumption will prevent them from fulfilling their task. One day, as one such future pastor was defending his role of giving people answers for their lives, he reached a turning point; a fellow student simply asked, "How is that going for you?" The student admitted that people rarely followed his advice, and eventually, he reframed his perspective. He began to use his insightfulness to help people find *their own* best solutions. He was beginning to understand the essence of this approach.

Practice, Practice

Another important lesson from participants has been their emphasis on practice as an important aspect of their training with the Solution-Focused model. In particular, they helped me realize that the best way to teach good listening skills was to allow them to practice listening to each other—rather than listening to me lecture on the importance of listening. I heard that feedback as a

5. Holland, "Constructing Helpful Conversations" 25.
6. Holland, "Constructing Helpful Conversations," 25.

suggestion to devote more time to practice, and now I regularly schedule sessions where they take turns counseling each other. Emphasizing our commitment to confidentiality, I also stress that they should only talk about situations from their own lives that they are comfortable discussing. In practicing with each other, trainees gain experience as counselor *and* counselee. Especially in this latter capacity, they have the chance to witness first-hand the validity of the Solution-Focused model, as they often receive help with their own problems.

While some are intimidated at first, the trainees also find it very helpful to make video recordings of their practice sessions, which we then watch together. As we view their work, we use Solution-Focused questions: we ask them to notice what they did well, what they were thinking as they were listening, and what exceptions they notice in areas where they struggle. These opportunities to observe their work are highlights for me as the instructor. I see the students becoming more and more comfortable using the model and coming to believe that they can be helpful to others. As one participant stated, "[W]ithout practice at doing this I would lack confidence."[7]

Know the Theory of the Model

I encourage those who are new to the Solution-Focused perspective to read beyond this work. Certainly, that can include more instruction about the practice and techniques of the model, but reading for a theoretical background is even more important. An understanding of the theories of postmodern therapies provides an important frame of reference for training others in the Solution-Focused model. Being theoretically grounded in the writings of foundational postmodern authors—Gregory Bateson, Kenneth Gergen, Brad Keeney, Peter DeJong, Insoo Kim Berg, Steve De Shazer, Michael White, and others—contributes more to my teaching than anything else I've done.

7. Holland, "Constructing Helpful Conversations," 28.

Students regularly ask me for resources on these concepts that are written from a Christian faith perspective. My own experience is that while there are a few good resources in that regard, Howard Stone's perspective is accurate: "Most pastoral counseling writers, unfortunately, have eschewed these new methods and pursued seemingly endless variations of early-twentieth century therapeutic approaches."[8] As quoted earlier, Stone goes on to observe, "While theory and practice in psychology, psychotherapy, and marriage and family therapy since that time have evolved to reflect new research and changing social conditions, it almost seems that the pastoral counseling field has 'fixated' (if I may use a Freudian term) on its beginnings, its theory developmentally stuck, as it were, in a therapeutic model of an earlier era."[9]

In teaching the theoretical concepts of counseling in seminary, I ask students to read works by secular authors like those above because I believe they offer the best perspectives. I also believe that, as seminary students, they are learning good theology. With good theology, they will have the perspectives they need for applying these ideas in ministry and in faith. I also emphasize the work discussed in chapter 2 by Deborah Van Deusen Hunsinger on the integration of theology and psychology. In her view, integration is "not a theoretical desideratum, but a skill to be developed by the ecclesial practitioner (in the context of pastoral counseling.)"[10] I propose that this praxis of integration is foremost an aesthetic endeavor, energized by the Holy Spirit and personalized in the caregiver who, by studying the best of theology and of psychology, develops the skills of good counseling.

Provide Regular Supervision

One of the keys to maintaining the ministry of lay caregivers is ongoing training and opportunities for them to reflect on their

---

8. Stone, "Congregational Setting of Pastoral Counseling," 187.
9. Stone, "Congregational Setting of Pastoral Counseling," 187.
10. Hunsinger, *Postliberal Theology*, 52.

experiences. I encourage supervisors to have regular conversations with trainees that, within the ethical boundaries of confidentiality, allow trainees to process the work they are doing. The practicum for my degree in Marriage and Family Therapy included four semesters of weekly meetings with supervisors to give reports of our counseling sessions, discuss the work we were doing, and particularly, discuss cases with which we were struggling. Using the Solution-Focused perspective, my supervisors listened intently, asked good questions, believed that we were the "experts" on the counseling we were doing, and helped us find our own solutions for going forward in our work. In my early meetings with supervisors, wanting to convince them I was doing good work, I only brought my successes to supervision. But because their style of supervision was to honor the work we were doing, I soon learned that rather than trying to impress them, my best use of supervision was to bring them the cases with which I was truly struggling. Now, in my own work guiding trainees, I strive to follow that empowering approach of helping students find their best skills for even the most challenging cases.

I also learned the importance of having supervisors to whom I could turn when I faced an ethical challenge or wondered about a dual relationship. In one instance, I became concerned that a counselee was attracted to me. In a quick phone call before the next session, my supervisor masterfully helped me to find a way to change the interpersonal dynamics with the counselee. I decided that encouraging her to invite her husband to our next session might reframe our relationship—while also benefiting her marriage. Having a resource like my supervisor is particularly important for lay caregivers who, as members of the congregation and also representatives of the church, will need help and accountability for managing dual relationships well.

Conclusion

THIS BOOK HAS BEEN about helping caregivers to have good conversations with people in distress. I believe that in training others for good conversations, we help people live their lives from the best parts of themselves, rather than from the broken places. By training caregivers to respect and honor people as experts in their own lives and to believe that people are doing—at least from their perspectives—what they think is best, we model for them what it is like to respect each other. We can provide a safe place for people to express their feelings honestly. We can affirm that life and relationships are difficult and often painful, but that when individuals undergo difficulties or are hurt by others, what they do next is what matters. We can help them to forgive and to restore their connections. We can help families and individuals construct more reasonable, less self-centered definitions of what it means to be happy, and of what they can expect from each other. We can help people see that not being perfect doesn't mean they are failures.

Howard Stone writes, "When it comes to guiding people through life's difficulties and crises, America's clergy have long been—and still are—at the front lines."[1] Statistics consistently report that when they have personal problems, the majority of people turn to a minister for counsel. But the minister does not have to carry all the responsibility by herself. Another aspect of the minister's task is to equip others for ministry. By preparing mature congregational

---

1. Stone, "Congregational Setting of Pastoral Counseling," 181.

members to have good conversations, we help our church members to bear each other's burdens.

My goal in writing has been to offer a sound and practical model for training caregivers, which I believe is important. I also know that while preparation and useful techniques may be beneficial to that work, what matters most is not what caregivers learn but who they are. It is important that they have their own lives in order as much as possible—but there is more to it than that. I believe that the task of working with others to solve problems begins in the good news of the Christian gospel. As Glen Boyd observes, "Our ultimate relatedness to God takes place in the context of radical non-pathologizing grace in which God accepts us without judgment, even with a DSM-IV diagnosis. God-in-Christ participates with us in a hope-filled conversation toward salvation and wholeness."[2] Mary Pipher says that when counseling "succeeds, it is a miracle. It is the result of the caring, respectful connection of people working together to solve problems. It is a fine human endeavor, as worthy of respect as a good poem, a symphony or field goal."[3]

The responsibility of trying to make a difference in the midst of the turmoil of people's lives is a demanding challenge, but if we are going to bear one another's burdens, it is a challenge we are all called to face. As we accept this challenge, we can find peace and empowerment knowing that "in the beginning was the word,"[4] a word that has always been speaking order out of chaos. And sometimes, in surprising and mysterious ways, God uses us to continue that word—to talk, to listen, and to gently guide people toward the redeeming presence of God. Rather than diagnosing and pathologizing the human dilemma, my hope is that we may all learn the language of the good news, which liberates those who are imprisoned by oppressive words and sets them free into the love and mercy of a caring God.

2. Boyd, "Kerygma and Conversation," 161.
3. Pipher, *Shelter of Each Other*, 139.
4. John 1:1.

Bibliography

Adamowicz, Michael W. "Diagnostic and Statistical Manual of Mental Disorders." https://www.mentalhelp.net/articles/diagnostic-and-statistical-manual-of-mental-disorders/.

Adams, Jay E. "What Is Nouthetic Counseling?" http://www.nouthetic.org/what-is-nouthetic-counseling.

American Psychiatric Association. *Diagnostic and Statistical Manual of Mental Disorders*. 5th ed. Arlington, VA: American Psychiatric, 2013.

Anderson, Harlene, and Harold A. Goolishian. "Beyond Cybernetics: Comments on Atkinson and Heath's 'Further Thoughts on Second-Order Family Therapy.'" *Family Process* 29 (1990) 157–63.

———. "The Client is the Expert: A Not Knowing Approach to Therapy." In *Therapy as Social Construction*, edited by Sheila McNamee and Kenneth J. Gergen, 25–39. Newbury Park, CA: Sage, 1992.

Anderson, Harlene, and Harold A. Goolishian. "Beyond Cybernetics: Comments on Atkinson and Heath's 'Further Thoughts on Second-Order Family Therapy.'" *Family Process* 29 (1990) 157–63.

Bateson, Gregory. *Steps to an Ecology of Mind*. Chicago: University of Chicago Press, 1972.

Bateson, Gregory, et al. "Toward a Theory of Schizophrenia." *Behavioral Science* 1 (1956) 251–64.

Bonhoeffer, Dietrich. *Life Together*. New York: Harper & Row, 1954.

Boyd, Glenn E. "Kerygma and Conversation." *Journal of Pastoral Care* 50.2 (1996) 161–69.

Brock, Gregory. *American Association for Marriage and Family Therapy Ethics Casebook*. 2nd ed. Washington, D.C.: American Association for Marriage and Family Therapy, 1998.

Camenisch, Paul. "Clergy Ethics and the Professional Ethics Model." In *Clergy Ethics in a Changing Society: Mapping the Terain*, edited by James P. Wind, 114–33. Louisville: Westminister, 1991.

Carter, John D., and Bruce Narramore. *The Integration of Psychology and Theology: An Introduction*. Grand Rapids: Zondervan, 1979.

BIBLIOGRAPHY

Council for Accreditation of Counseling & Related Educational Programs. http://www.cacrep.org.

Crabb, Larry. *Basic Principles of Biblical Counseling*. Grand Rapids: Zondervan, 1975.

———. *Effective Biblical Counseling: A Model for Helping Caring Christians Become Capable Counselors*. Grand Rapids: Zondervan, 1977.

De Jong, Peter, and Insoo Kim Berg. *Interviewing for Solutions*. Pacific Grove, CA: Brooks/Cole, 2002.

Dowd, E. Thomas. "Stasis and Change in Cognitive Psychotherapy: Client Resistance and Reactance as Mediating Variables." In *Cognitive Psychotherapy: Stasis & Change*, edited by Windy Dryden and Peter Trower, 139–58. New York: Springer, 1989.

Epstein, Eugene S., and Victor E. Loos. "Some Irreverent Thoughts on the Limits of Family Therapy: Toward a Language-Based Explanation of Human Systems." *Journal of Family Psychology* 2.4 (1989) 405–21.

Foucault, Michel. *Power/Knowledge: Selected Interviews and Other Writings*. New York: Pantheon, 1980.

Freedman, Jill, and Gene Combs. *Narrative Therapy: The Social Construction of Preferred Realities*. New York: Norton, 1996.

Fruggeri, Laura. "Therapeutic Process as the Social Construction of Change." In *Inquiries in Social Construction*, edited by Sheila McNamee and Kenneth J. Gergen, 40–53. Thousand Oaks, CA: Sage, 1992.

Gergen, Kenneth J. *The Saturated Self: Dilemmas of Identity in Contemporary Life*. New York: Basic, 1991.

Gerkin, Charles V. *An Introduction to Pastoral Care*. Nashville: Abingdon, 1997.

Gula, Richard. *Ethics in Pastoral Ministry*. Mahwah, NJ: Paulist, 1996.

———. *Just Ministry: Professional Ethics for Pastoral Ministers*. Mahwah, NJ: Paulist, 2010.

Hoffman, Lynn. "A Reflexive Stance for Family Therapy." *Journal of Strategic and Systemic Therapies* 10.3–4 (1991) 4–17.

Holland, Jack. "Constructing Helpful Conversations: Solution-Focused Lay Pastoral Care in a Local Congregation." *Family and Community Ministries: Empowering Through Faith*. 22.2 (2007) 22–30.

Howe, Leroy. *A Pastor in Every Pew: Equipping Laity for Pastoral Care*. Valley Forge, PA: Judson, 2000.

Hunsinger, George. "Postliberal Theology." In *The Cambridge Companion to Postmodern Theology*, edited by Kevin J. Vanhoozer, 42–57. Cambridge University Press, 2003.

Illouz, Eva. "How Therapy Became a Multimillion Dollar Industry." *Haaretz Israel News*, June 4, 2012. http://www.haaretz.com/israel-news/how-therapy-became-a-multimillion-dollar-industry-1.436431.

———. *Saving the Modern Soul: Therapy, Emotions, and the Culture of Self-Help*. Berkeley: University of California Press, 2008.

Johnson, Eric L., and Stanton L. Jones. *Psychology and Christianity: Four Views*. Downers Grove, IL: InterVarsity, 2000.

Jones, Stanton L., and Richard E. Butman. *Modern Psycotherapies: A Comprehensive Christian Appraisal.* Downers Grove, IL: InterVarsity, 1991.

Kollar, Charles Allen. *Solution-Focused Pastoral Counseling.* Grand Rapids: Zondervan, 1997.

Korzybski, Alfred. *Science and Sanity: An Introduction to Non-Aristotelian Systems and General Semantics.* Englewood, NJ: Institute of General Semantics, 1995.

Kudlac, Karen E. "Including God in the Conversation: The Influence of Religious Beliefs on the Problem-Organized System." *Family Therapy* 18.3 (1991) 277–85.

Lampe, Karen. *The Caring Congregation: Training Manual and Resource Guide.* Nashville: Abingdon, 2014.

Murashko, Alex. "Pastors Urged to Sign Newly Released Code of Ethics." *Christian Post,* June 14, 2012. https://www.christianpost.com/news/pastors-urged-to-sign-newly-released-code-of-ethics.html.

National Center on Birth Defects and Developmental Disabilities. "Attention-Deficit/Hyperactivity Disorder (ADHD)." https://www.cdc.gov/ncbddd/adhd/diagnosis.html.

Oden, Thomas C. *Care of Souls in the Classic Tradition.* Minneapolis: Fortress, 1984. https://www.religion-online.org/book/care-of-souls-in-the-classic-tradition/.

Parent, Miriam Stark. "Boundaries and Roles in Ministry Counseling." *American Journal of Pastoral Counseling* 8.2 (2006) 1–25.

Pipher, Mary. *The Shelter of Each Other.* New York: Ballantine, 1997.

Pope, Benjamin. *The Mental Health Interview.* New York: Pergamon, 1979.

Privette, Gayle, et al. "Preferences for Religious or Nonreligious Counseling and Psychotherapy." *Psychological Reports* 75.1, pt. 2 (1994) 539–46.

Real, Terry. "The Therapeutic Use of Self in Constructionist/Systemic Therapy." *Family Process* 29.3 (1990) 255–72.

Roberts, Robert C. *Taking the Word to Heart: Self & Other in an Age of Therapies.* Grand Rapids: Wm. B. Eerdmans, 1993.

Schnarch, David M. *Constructing the Sexual Crucible: An Integration of Sexual and Marital Therapy.* New York: Norton, 1991.

"The State of Mental Health in America." http://www.mentalhealthamerica.net/issues/state-mental-health-america.

Stephen Ministries. https://www.stephenministries.org/default.cfm.

Stone, Howard W. "The Congregational Setting of Pastoral Counseling: A Study of Pastoral Counseling Theorists from 1949–1999." *Journal of Pastoral Care* 55.2 (February 2001) 181–96.

Stortz, Martha Ellen. *PastorPower.* Nashville: Abingdon, 1993.

Szasz, Thomas S. *The Myth of Mental Illness: Foundations of a Theory of Personal Conduct.* New York: Harper & Row, 1974.

Tan, Siang-Yang. *Lay Counseling: Equipping Christians for a Helping Ministry.* Grand Rapids: Zondervan, 1991.

———. "The Role of the Psychologist in Paraprofessional Helping." *Professional Psychology: Research and Practice* 28.4 (August 1997) 368–72.

Thomas, Frank N., and Jack Cockburn. *Competency-Based Counseling: Building on Client Strengths*. Minneapolis: Fortress, 1998.

Van Deusen Hunsinger, Deborah. "An Interdisciplinary Map for Christian Counselors." In *Care for the Soul*, edited by Mark R. McMinn and Timothy R. Phillips. Downers Grove, IL: InterVarsity, 2001.

———. *Theology and Pastoral Counseling: A New Interdisciplinary Approach*. Grand Rapids: Wm. B. Eerdmans, 1997.

Vine's Greek New Testament Dictionary. http://gospelhall.org/bible/bible.php?search=phortion&dict=vine&lang=greek.

Von Foerster, Heinz. "Ethics and Second-Order Cybernetics." *Stanford Electronic Humanities Review* 4.2 (1995). https://web.stanford.edu/group/SHR/4-2/text/foerster.

Von Glasersfeld, Ernst. *Radical Constructivism: A Way of Knowing and Learning*. Washington, D.C.: Falmer, 1995.

Wampold, Bruce E. *The Great Psychotherapy Debate: Models, Methods, and Findings*. Mahwah, NJ: Lawrence Erlbaum Associates, 2001.

Wang, Philip S., et al. "Patterns and Correlates of Contacting Clergy for Mental Disorders in the United States." *Health Services Research* 38.2 (April 2003) 647–73.

Watzlawick, Paul, et al. *Pragmatics of Human Communication: A Study of Interactional Patterns, Pathologies, and Paradoxes*. New York: Norton, 1967.

White, Michael, and David Epston. *Narrative Means to Therapeutic Ends*. New York: Norton, 1990.

www.ingramcontent.com/pod-product-compliance
Lightning Source LLC
Chambersburg PA
CBHW070502090426
42735CB00012B/2654